AF553764

Rural Tension in India

Rural Tension in India

ANIL KANT MISHRA
Department of Sociology,
R.M. College, Saharsa, Bihar.

1998
Discovery Publishing House
New Delhi-110002

First Published-1998

ISBN 81-7141-416-8

Published by:
Discovery Publishing House
4831/24, Ansari Road, Prahlad Street,
Daryaganj, New Delhi-110002 *(INDIA)*
Phone: 3279245
Fax: 91-11-3253475

Printed at:
Tarun Offset Printers

Contents

Acknowledgements

The obligations incurred in the preparation of this book have been many and so my thanks go first of all to the people of the village. I am grateful for the patience they have shown in attending to problem. Needless to write, this book could never have been written without their co-operation. First of all I express my gratitude to late Sri Rajiv Gandhi, former Prime Minister of India, who through his Radio broadcast invited the social thinkers attention to this social tension created by economic unrest in rural India. I could not have undertaken this area of interest if he had not invited like this.

I am profoundly grateful to my friends, collegues and relatives from whom I have received liberal help in completing this book particularly to my brother Sri D.K.Mishra (Engineer), and my sister Asha Rani Pathak, M.A. (sociology) L.L.B.

I am also indebted to my father, Sri Sunder Kant Mishra and my father-in-law, Sri S. Jha for helping me by going through the manuscripts and holding meaningful discussion on certain topics.

It is difficult for me to express my gratefulness in words to my wife, Usha, who has contributed in many tangible and intangible ways—by her support, companionship and advice in writing this book. My two sons Aushu and Abhinav always help me in writing this book so express my love to them.

There are also others who have helped me in bringing out this book particularly Dr. R.R.Prasad, Director, Faculty of Sociology National Institute of Rural Development. I express my heartfelt gratitude to them and especially to Dr. R.R. Prasad.

Several institutions have earned my gratitude for making it possible for me to consult books and journals related to this book. In this regard I would like to mention the Indian Institute of Advanced Study, Shimla, J.N.U. libirary, A.N. Sinha Institute of Social Studies, Patna.

Anil Kant Mishra

Preface

In ancient time India was called a "Golden Bird". This epithet was given to our country by the foreigners because of its affluence, prosperity and over all peace and harmony. But as time rolled on this scene started changing. The pyramid based on social hierachy with its fascinating festoons of many castes, creeds and customs started showing signs of cracks. Now the scene has so much changed that the social thinkers have felt obliged to diagnose and possibly suggest remedies for the ills that are disintegrating the social fabric.

The need to cope with tensions and strains is a universal need not limited to modern society. Nevertheless, it seems plausible that modern urban industrial society, with its high level of complexity and interdependence generates particular types of tensions and strains that differ from the tensions and strains of simpler societies.

Now Rural India is in ferment, conflict, confusion, disharmony and consequent violence seems to have taken entire nation in its firm grip. The over-all result of this turmoil is tension, powerful and all-embrassing.

During the last decade the cure of social tension has abruptly registered an upward swing owing due to caste conflict, land grabbing naxal and its allied movements are just off shoots of this social tension. From North to South or East to West an invisible thread of social tension seems to be coursing, through the entire nation. The conflict between the landed peassantry and the landless people, between the so called high caste and low caste, between the privileged few and the non-privileged mass, between achievement and sky-rocketing aspiration the scene is similar with insignificant local variations noted sociologist Yogendra Singh has also presented the rural scene like this "The relationship between these peasant and the landless workers became more pugnacious and exploitative with the rise in their economic and political influence and power. This is reflected in increased incidence of conflict between landless workers and farmers in different parts of the country. It led to increased caste-class tensions in villagers "(Social Change in India: 1993: 30)".

In this present study it has been tried to study, anatomise and trace the rural tension on the economic perspective. I have also tried to go deep in to this economic aspect of rural tension,to that a theory of rural tension is established. I am quite sure the factors unravelled through this study which commonly escape the notice of the policy makers will help in formulating a full proof statergy for combating this cankerous civil in rural India.

In the present study I sampled out a village namely 'Bihara'in Saharsa district of north Bihar because it contains all the symtoms of tension caused by economic factors. In the recent past it has witnessed scenes of great clashes for ceiling land, land grabing share-cropping and wage. And it is quite obvious that the fire and fury of this tension has still not ebbed out.

The study is by no means comprehensive. It has limitations of methodology, area and data. Yet I fervently hope that the Indian social scientists will find enough food for their thought and they will feel enthused to solve the problem for giving a new, healthy and prosperous shape to tension-free rural India.

I am not sure of my success but even if I have succeed in creating a sparkle of interest in those who can metamorphose this rural scenes, I will feel amply rewarded.

Anil Kant Mishra

1 INTRODUCTION

Today, man lives under the strain of mounting tensions that affect every aspect of life whether personal, social, religious, political or economic. Perhaps, in no other period in the history of mankind were tensions so powerful and encompassing as in the present age. Every sphere of life has become depersonalised and unsurveyable and society disintegrated and unstable. The complicated social machinery has brought differentiation of functions which has led to the differences in claims for social recognition and privileges. Various large scale organizations lack adaptation to each other's function which results in the cancellation of each others affectiveness. Social stability is tried to be maintained by differentiation of classes. "There remain no basic, permanent values in social life: every thing is scattered, confused and disintegrated. The confusion of norms and values leads to the distruction of the network of socio-cultural relationship. "(Sorokin:Vol.III: 1937:500)

Japanese sociologists and others evidently working on the commission on tension from the Unesco, have recognised nine distinet groups of tensions in the society-

There are:

(1) Tensions in family life;
(2) Tensions within communities;
(3) Tensions between countries;
(4) Tensions around the problem of the 'Eta' (out castes);
(5) Racial tensions;
(6) Tensions in religious life;
(7) Tensions in economic life;
(8) Ideological tensions; and
(9) Tensions among young people.(Ghurye:1968:9)

In this way tensions constitute a serious threat to human existence. The word 'Tension' is an adaptation of Latin word ' Tensionem' (Noun of action, formed on 'tendere' to stretch: past participle, 'tenseus' tent-us). The term tension is used in various senses. In physics, it denotes a constrained condition of the particles of body when subjected to force acting in opposite directions, away from each other, thereby tending to draw them apart, and balanced by forces of cohesion holding them together. Here, it does not imply readiness to act but only to break nor docs it suggest the difficulty in restraining its actions towards an object. In Botany, it is applied to a strain of pressure in the cells or tissiues of plants in the course of growth. In Zoology, it means the contraction of muscles and a further meaning is added to the physical sense, since a taut muscle suggests difficulty in checking itself from action and thus involves a readiness to act. Similarly in physiology and pathology, it means the condition, in any part of the body, of being stretched and strained and a sensation indicating this feeling of tightness. When used figuratively, it means a straining of strained condition of mind, feeling or nerves.(Bernard:1951).

In psychology the term denotes "upsets in complacency or optimum balance on emotional unpheaval, being the principal charcteristics of hypertension." (The New Dictionary of Psychology:1947:327).

This disharmony or upset may result in restlessness, anxiety, instability, incoordination, hyper activity etc.(Kane:1951:663).

In general an organism is accommodated to a certain optimal level of external, stimuli. Any change in these stimuli produces disequilibrium or tension in the organism; the resulting tension involves, the conscious accompaniment of which is sensation. Motive implies tensions so that motivated behaviour is related to some sort of tension. Motivated behaviour is organised behaviour that shows a direction of efforts motives and tensions are so interrelated that in order to organise many small tensions into one unified pattern, the process of developing motive is followed. Thus in motivated behaviour many small tensions are managed. Even those tensions that have social, cultural or individual habits as their patterns may also be managed in the same way. The whole organism is an unstable equillibrium in relation to its environment, and represents an infinitely complex configuration or tensions, the more persistent of which are referred to as structures, attitudes, character. Since normal mental life oscillates between two extremes: a plan of action in which sensorimotor functions occur and a plan of dream, in which we live our imaginative life, of which memory is major part, there are as many corresponding intermediate planes as there are degrees of 'attention of life' adaption to reality. The mind has a power sui-generies to produce contractions and expansions of itself thereby calling attention to the need of distinguising various heights of tension of tones in psychic life.

Interprets the life of the universe and the life of human personality in terms of tension, (*The Dictionary of Philosophy*: 315).

In social and political thinking the term 'Tension' means an attitude of hostility among persons or groups towards each other, expressing itself in strained relationship which may break or rupture.(Avasthi:1973:5)

Tensions have been defined as the act of stretching the condition of being stretched light or mental strain or any strained relations as between government. (College Standard Dictionary:120 as quoted Sachchidananda and Iyer: 1969)

It is thc emotional concomitant of something else, for the 'Uneasiness' and ' mental strain must have source, and something, presumably relations' must be 'stretched' or 'strained' to give rise to the conflict and uncertainty implied by emotinal reaction. Change, in the sense of any challenge to the status quo appear to be the central factor in the emergence of tension, for a given social arrangement or more or less accomodation a situation of intergroup antagonism, in any disruption or stable expectations with reference to intergroup conduct can be expected to lead to an increase in tension. Whenever one group ceases to acquiesce or presses for a change in previous accepted social patterns while the other group wishes to maintain them without being sure of their ability to do so, these exists the typical setting in which conflict and the possibility of violence emerge. The doubt, strain, uncertanty and concern over the outcome of the conflict, the uneasiness experienced over the possible course of events, make up the subjective experience of the conflict refered to as tension. (Sachchidananda and Iyer:1969).

Tension results from discrepancies between people's actual situation and their needs and goals. Therefore, the motivation to drop out of a complex and highly interdependent society and to establish a simpler self sufficient community in perhaps a response to the particular tensions and strains experienced in a large complex society. (Paul:1981:539-540). Tensions level can be raised by economic distress or by other kind or social maladjustment. (Ghurye: 1968:8).

R.M.MacIver in his valuable text book on sociology 'Society' brings in inter group tensions and tells that the phenomena of prejudice, tension and discrimination between groups an extremely variable.

There are some views which deal the causes of intergroup tension to external circumstances. Some explain that the lack of coordination and prevalence of contradictions among various groups in society causes tension, both in individual as well as in group life. Robin M.Williams (1947:60) explains that the possibility of intergroup tension and mass violence is greatest in—

(1) Prolonged frustration leading to a high tension level.
(2) Presence of population elements with a propensity of violence.
(3) A highly visible and rapid change in intergroup relations.
(4) A precipitating incident of intergroup conflict.

R.M.Williams profiting by the discussion of Coser and Korchin and the sociologist T. Parsons as in the approaches to national unity by L.Bryson and others has defined some of the basic concepts involved in the topic of, tension. Leaving out 'group' prejudice' 'Discrimination' and competition and 'aggression' Williams noted substance of the definition of group hostility reserving that of 'conflict' for the next section where it properly belongs. Groups hostility is shared and common attitude, shown of seen in verbal and or non-verbal acts, which discharge,insult, ostracize,threaten and or injure members of social group towards which hostility is entertained. Intergroup hostitity is conditioned to a large extent by the level of tension in a society. The tension level of any social grouping is in part a function of the realtive emphasis in the group's culture upon participation in common values as over against individual or group acquisition of scarce goods.(Williams:1947:4-5).For further discussion in tension or social tension it is important to know the concept of frustration and conflict, or which is precondition of tension or social tension.

It is universally accepted that frustrations have always been inevitable in human life. Talking about the significant role of frustation Rosenzweiz says, " Frustration is such a universal aspect of experience that some philosophers have even woven an entire metaphysical system around it."(Rosenzweiz:1947:905).

The diagram on page 9, shows the motivated behaviour directed towards a goal encounters barriers in the physical or psychological frustration is the result.

Its inevetability also consists in the fact that frustration is closely related of the problem of adjustment, change, personality development or growth. In all social strata and in all phases of personality development each one of us is bound to face repeatedly with the problem of frustrations.There is some force or motivalion behind all behaviour,which activates the individual for achieving the goal. When motivated behaviour is blocked by an obstacle, tension is produced and it lasts as long as the barrier is present. In this connection Murphy speaks 'Frustration is the blockage of a path to a goal, tension is kept high. (Murphy: 1947:144-145).

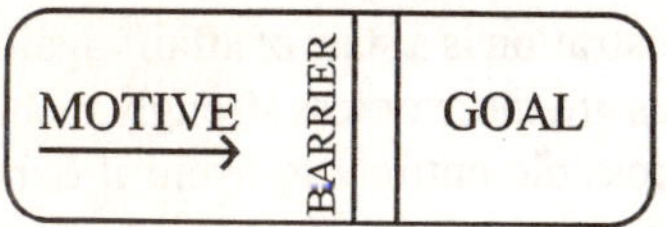

(Arrow, in the above diagram shows the derection of the motivated behaviour towards a goal, the vertical lines in the middle of the diagram, show the ensoluble barriers, which results in frustration.)

A part from above discussion on frustration some of the typical explanations have been made on frustration 'The denial or thwarting of motives by obstacles which lie between needs and goals' (Ruch:1955:596), the blocking of or interference with on going motivated behaviour. The emotional state resulting from being blocked, thwarted or defeated (Sauford:1961:412), is a situation in which a person's on going motivated behaviour or his organised man of action is temporarily or permanently prevented from reaching consummation (Cameron:1947:130),"State inferral to exist when deviant behaviour is observed as result of blocking of or interfereuce with goal directed behaviour" (Underwood:1949:628)

"The condition which exists when goal-response suffers interference" (Dollard:1944:11), any inference with a goal response or with the instrumental acts leading to it (Seas:1945:215),

"The condition resulting from interference with a goal response (Adams:1940:158)," the blocking or interference of the satisfaction of an aroused need in rough some barrier or obstruction (Symonds:1946:51), "the blocking of drive evoked behaviour (Davitz:1942:310),"the condition of being thwarted in the satisfaction of a motive (Harsiman 1947:143)Maier(1940:540) defines frustration in more dynamic terms 'We prefer to limit the term frustration to designate the slate where continued failure causes tearing function to cease operating and other mechanisms of adjustment to begin operation a frustration is said to be any interference with some on going goal directed activity (Berkowitz:1962:1) "when motivated behaviour is blocked before it can achieve its goal" (Smith:1958:55).

Barker (1941:386)points to the subjectivity of frustration, as he says "by a frustrating situation will be meant any situation in which an obstacle physical, social, or conceptual, personal or environmental— prevent the satisfaction of a desire, it includes only those situations where the subject himself accepts the obstacle as impassable, the solution as impossible. For Mowrer(1938:129) frustration is an antithesis to happiness to quote his own words, "Frustration is a state of affairs against which the affected individual's energies are more or less strongly mobilised which he seeks to eliminate or if possible entirely to avoid if happiness may fairly be said to represent the ultimate goal of all human endeavour, frustration is its antithesis. According to Krech and Crutchfield (1962:134),frustration is the motivational and emotional state which results from persistent blockage of goal directed behaviour. It may lead the individual change in cognition to maladaptive behaviour.

It is universally accepted that frustrations have always been inevitable in human life and are more or less in the present age. The human being in spite of being the crown of creation remains a small frail organism with limited capacities, physical as well as mental. He constantly strives towards goals which gratify his complicated biological and physiological needs. Sometime these are achieved with relative case, but a large number of needs and and motives inevitably remain unsatisfied or only partly satisfied due to some obstacle lying between need and its goal. When the obstacle becomes difficult to over come, it creates frustration.

Research on frustration, aggression and tension makes it clear that which is frustrating depends upon the goals and intention of the persons supposedly being frustrated. Those goals may not be evident to the observer. All this still does not deny that a person or a group of persons, feeling frustrated, may attack another group that is a safe and exciting target but is unrelated to the frustration. Freud(1915) was one of the first of emphasise and analyse in detail the points of frustration that when a person is prevented from satisfying his needs. He is likely to engage in aggression behaviour. Early experimented work (Dollard:1944)on this hypothesis provided some support for it. Often the frustrating agent is not a suitable target for hostility because of his great power. In such instances the hostility may be directed against a scapegoat. On innocent party. There is such envidence to indicate that the blocking of goal-directed behaviour frequently creates hostile implses in the indivitual as well as in group.

G.S. Ghurye, noted sociologist of India observe's "Conflict is a concept inseparably connected with tension" (Ghury: 1968:50). But it does not mean that tension and conflict are the synonymous terms infact these two terms differ from each other. Rajendra Avasthi (1973:5-6) observes though tension may lead to conflict and conflict may produce tension. Tension which is a trained or tant condition does not imply actual clash between the entagoniss,though it may involve a preparation for clash; conflict singly actual clash between the antagonist. A conflict is a struggle, a mutually distructive realationship of the individual or group in which the immediate aims of the oponents are to neutralize, injure or eleminate their rivals or to threat each other's interests or purpose.

In this way frustration, tension and conflict are interelated phenomena. Any type of social tension increases if there is wide gulf between the hierarchieal ideals and the prevailing social realites or if the disparity in the cultural conditions of the various strata of hierarchieal society is so great as to eclipse the common social purposes. The possibility of inter group conflict and social tension also increases with the speed in which changes take place, since they nccessitate rapid adjustment on the part of the individuals no sooner have the individuals regulated their behaviour to adjust themselves to the new conditions than they are again forced with problem of readjustment. Consequently, the permanent and stable expecations of intergroup behavioural patterns are disrupted. This rapidity in social change may to a certain extent, be attributed to the advancement of technology in economic sphere which breeds social tension in many other ways also.

Extension of social relationship on the basis of any discrimination leads to terrible social tension and hostility. Hostility towards different groups arises if the sense of insecurity, out of the feeling that the other groups are the threat to one's existance as a member of small group or exterior groups.

Post independent India has witnessed considerable transformation in the agrarian relations due to the introduction of numerous institutional reforms. The abolition of zamindari, the imposition of ceiling on land, steps taken for agricultural labourers, and the consolidation of fragmented holding are some of the important steps in this direction. They have brought about radical changes in the agrarian social structure. Eventually the rich and middle land owers have directly been pitted against the marginal formers, share-croppers and landless labourers making it endemie phenomenon in India today.

The growing agrarians tension and violence in different parts of the country has thus received the attention of social scientists and administrators alike. The prime concern of social scientists has been with the patterns of inequality and conflict as they occur due to the changing land relations wheras administrators have studied the law and order problem involved in such conflicts.

It has been observed that the discrepancy between the egalitarian social norms and conservative distribution norms upheld by the prosperous and dominent sections of society is the primary cause of agrarian unrest. It has also been observed in the rural scenario that the perception of prevalance of disparities in income by the rural poor, a viable numeral strength of the agricultural labour forces and their consciousness of their right, the existence of adequate support structure provided by political parties. These are the conditions which indicate that India is in Tension.

In the present book it has been tried to elaborate how the economic factors create social tension in rural India. This book is based on localised study on the intenive micro field work. For field work a village namely 'Bihara' of Bihar state which falls in Saharsa District has been selected as case study. 'Bihara village is a tension and conflict prone village. Land conflict, labour conflict, atrocities on Harijan and santhal conflict between and haves and have nots have been seen in this village. Technique like direct interview, non-participant observation has been used. Tool for data collection was schedule, each family head is the unit of sample. Two hundred household heads have been selected in this empirical study.

Objective of this present work is :-

1) To find out the gravity of social tension on the basis of economic factors.
2) To give some of the suggestion for removal of social tension on the basis of economic factors at rural India.

•

2 AN OVERVIEW OF AREA UNDER STUDY

As it has been written that this empirical field work is related to rural areas. In this empirical field work a conflict and tension prone village 'Bihara; (falls in Saharsa district of north Bihar) has been selected for sample village. Before any discussion of Bihara village it is essential to know about India, The state of Bihar and Saharsa in which this village falls.

India is the the seventh biggest country in the world in size. She has an area of about 32,68000 square kilometers. She covers only 2 persent of the total land area in the world.

In 1991, the population of India was counted to be about 844 million. She holds about 14 persent of the total population of the world.

With only 2 percent of the total land she has 14 percent of the total population. So, average population density is seven times that of the world. India's average population per square kilometer is 267 persons.

People of different races have been coming to India at different times. But they all have intermixed with Indian people and culture. The Indian culture is very tolerant and accommodating. So we have people with different religions, speaking different languages. They follow different social customs and being to different castes. India has the composite population and composite culture from Kashmir to Kanya Kumari, NEFA to Rann of Kutch. Population of India is mostly rural.

The distribution of population of India is very uneven. There are parts that are very thickly populated. Also there are parts that are moderately thickly populated. This is because of the differences in climate, soil and productivity, high mountains and deserts have a sparse population. Plateaus and moderately fertile areas have medium population. The most thickly populated areas in India are Kerala and West Bengal. Thickly populated areas include the northern plain, the deltas of the Caveri, Krishna, Godavari, Mahanadi and Gujarat. Moderately populated areas are the southern platean and Malwa platean. Thinly populated aread are western Rajasthan, Rann of Kutch, Jammu and Kashmir, Himachal Pradesh, Kumoun hills in U.P. Arunachal Pradesh, Nagaland, Sikkim, Mizoram and Manipur.

About 55% of total land area is under the plough. The land is primary source of wealth of a country. The land of India is considerably fertile and the country possesses a lot of water resources for irrigation. About 70% of Indian working population works on farms and so India is chiefly an agricultural country. Agriculture is infact, the main stay of economy of India. Rice, Wheel, Millets, maize, pulses, oilseeds, sugar cane, tea, coffee, spices, cotton, jute, tobacco, Rubber and Fruits are produced in India.

Bihar is a state of dichotomies, split by geography, peoples and history. Twenty six centuries ago it become the seat of India's first empire, a center of progressive thinking and interprise. For over a thousand years it remained the nucleus of northern Indian civilization. Now, unfortunately it is the site of some of the country's worst conditions: over population, poverty, unemployment, low wage rate, low per capita income and violence.

Buddha loved and preached most of his life in rural Bihar. In the sixth century B.C., Pataliputra became the capital of the Magadhans and subsequently of the Mauryans and of other later great empires that promoted Buddhist culture, art-theater and literature, founded universities and encouraged open thought. After 600 A.D. Bihar lost its far-reaching power and its kingdoms become fragmented, but its newfound introspection gave impetus to the development of rural cultures and to the restrengthening of indegenous Hinduism. Invaders from Karnataka. in the eleventh century, founded a kingdom in north Bihar in which there evolved a unigue synthesis of southern and northern Indian customs and thought. The muslims, arriving in the twelfth century, annihilated most of the Buddhists, universities and institutions. The ruler Akbar made Bihar an integral part of the Mughal empire in the sixteenth century, and the state remined vital during the British reign. The farms of North Bihar supplied the British with opium and indigo the former used to secure Chinese trade rights and the latter a main stay of western and eastern textile production.

Contemporary Bihar has a reputation for conservatism, for reluctance to change. There is not as much concern for modenization in this state as in most others and as a results it has less public transporation, less electricity and fewer pucca roads in rural areas. Most districts are stagnant economicaly.

The only resource for the majority of North Biharis is rice cultivation, which is often insufficient to support the population of Bihar. The most widely spoken language is Hindi.Geographically Bihar has been divided into two regions i.e. north Bihar and South Bihar.

North Bihar is flat and criss-crossed with rivers, bounded by the foot hills of the Himalayas and Nepal on the north and by the wide Ganges River on the south. Social mobility is restricted, and the most prominent castes are Yadav (Previously cow and Buffolow herders, now mostly farmers), Brahmin, Rajput, Kayasths, Kurmi, Bhumihar and harijans.Dissatisfaction with economic and social conditions has engendered violence throughout north Bihar (Huyler:1985)

South Bihar is primarily a hilly plateau covered with dense forest. Historically it has been relatively inaccessible to invaders and has thus provided ideal habitat for the tribes residing there. Bihar has India's third highest tribal population, most of whom live in south Bihar. South Bihar also contains the nation's largest supply of coal, its biggest iron and steel plant, and the site for a huge government products.

Despite huge mineral wealth most fertile and Bihar's percapita income G.D.P. has been the lowest. The state affairs has created socio-economic tension and gave birth to many violent movements specially in central and south Bihar; This has not only impeded pace of development in right direction but has also created such a jawing chasm which anly excellerated pace of focal multifaced development can bridge.

Saharsa— No authentic information is available as to the origin of the name of Saharsa district but there is a village at a distance of about 3 Kms.from the Saharsa railway station which is know as Saharsa. Prior to the formation of the district there were only the village of saharsa and a railway station of the name.(Choudhary:1954:1)

Saharsa was created a seprate district on the Ist April 1954. Formerly. Saharsa had no independent status and part of Saharsa was included in the old district of Monghyr, Tirhut and Bhagalpur. Saharsa was created as head quarters of Koshi division on 2nd Oct.1972. Now two subdivisons namely Madhepura and Supaul have been sliced off and formed two separate districts. As per district Magistrate of Saharsa the population of Saharsa district is 11 Lacs 31 thousand 6 hundred and 8 (1991). Now the Saharsa district is bounded on the north by Supaul district, south by Khagaria district on east by Madhepura district and on the west by Madhubani, Darbhanga and Samastipur district.

Saharsa district is the land of Mithila. Mithila was one of the earliest centres of the Brahmanical civilization in the east. It is the land where Janak ruled, Yajanvalkya legislated and Gautam meditated. Janak gathered at his court some other celebraties of knowledge. From the study of Satpath Brahmana and Brihadaranyak upanisid it appears that Mithila continued to be the centre of Aryan civilization for centries and its cultural contacts with Kuru Panchal country in those days was a reality. The standard of philosophical discussion in the court of Janak points to the great erudition and cultural tradition of Mithila. It had the unique privilege of being the birth place of Vardhamana Mahavir, apostle of non-violence, twenty fourth Thirthankar of Jainism.

When Magadh lost its importance, Mithila become the centre of cultural regenaration. Its contribution to the development of our national cultural is immense. Yajnavalkaya developed the Madhyanayal inskha of the Yajurveda and Yajnavalkaya smiriti is the bed rock of Mithila. It is also symbol of the Hindu law. Pandit Madan Mishra of Mithila was married to Bharati, sister of Kumaril Bhatta, a great scholar of Budishm. In his Naskarmasidhi Madan's impatience with human suffering finds elequent expression. His theory of Avidhyanivar is identical with Bhahamajnam of Janak. Vachespati Mishra, who followed Madan Mishra is equally conscious of suffering of humanity and he dedicated his whole life to expounding the view of the earlier thinkers on the problem of human welfare. The main aim of Mithila thinker was to regulate the daily life according to Brahminical rituals.

A passage as described by Yajnavalkya says that the path of duty can be known through the usages of Mithila. (Choudhary:1976:249).

There was a famous Jaharada of Apana in the Angutrap region where Buddha stayed for about a month and delivered some of his important sermons. It is very diffcult to identify the village or the region of Angutrap at the present moment but it can be said with some amount of certainty that the present dirstrict of Saharsa with some of its ancient sites formed an important part of that region.

Saharsa district was an important centre of the Tantras. The cult of Tara goddess whose temple situated at Mahishi, 16 K.M.S. West of

Saharsa town belived to be of Tibetan origin, has been very popular in the district. Mahishi has been a very famous seat of the Urgatara worship and is looked upon with greater everence by the people even today. The origin of Mithila tantricism may be traced to Mahishi (Choudhary:1976:24-25).

The village Mahishi is ancient and, according to commonly accepted legend, this was the place where Madan Mishra, the great philosopher of the 8th century A.D.Lived. Shankaracharya came from the south and had a philosophic discussion first with Madan Mishra and then with his wife Bharati Devi. There is a mound at Mihishi village which is pointed out as the site where the philosophic disscussion between Madan Mishra and Shankaṛacharya had taken place. (Choudhary:1976:490).

The village Kandaha 10 K.M West of Saharsa town, is famous for sun-temple. There are other temples also near the sun temple. The inscription on the temple has been desciphered. It is of the time of Narasimha Deva of the Oinwara dynasty. (Choudhary:1976:485) who was contemporary of Vidhyapathi. Mithila is known for the lyrical love songs of Vidayapathi the priceless heritage of which has never been forgotten.

Natural Division

The entire district lies north of the Ganga and is comprised of plains. The southern portion of the district in more fertile and more densely populated. The deposit left by the turbulent Koshi river has affected the fertility of the soil but progressive implementation of Koshi project has turned the district in to veritable granary. The property of the district had been affected by ravages of floods. After the construction of the koshi Barage and secred embankments the areas of this region are free from ravage of Koshi and the sandy tracts are being reclaimed. The land in the western part of the district in fall of marshy overgrowth, full of kans and pater(Jungles). A number of canals have been constructed under the Koshi project which provide irrigational facilites to this district. The most important river of the district is the Koshi. The Koshi is notorious for its vagaries and was known as 'Behar's River of Sorrow'. During the rainy season it swell inundates large tracts of the district. One such occasion was 6 Oct. 1984 when eastern Koshi embankment was breached near Hauhatta Block causing enormous loss of human lives, cattle heads and standing crops of this area. Besides these vast tracts of fertile agricultural lands were turned into sandy tracts, and badly disrupted, road and rail communication.

Climatic Conditions

The meteorological observatory of Saharsa itself gives us the picture of Saharsa district. The cold weather commences by about the middle of November when mercury begins to drop fairly rapidly. January is the coldest month. The days become warmer in March while the nights continue to be cool. Both day and night temperature beings to increase rapidly after the middle of March. March to May is the summer season. The rainy season extenda from June to September, October being the transitional month, April is the hotest month of the year when temperature sometimes rising up to 43 c.

Flora and Fauna

Paddy and wheat are grown in the alluvial and reclaimed soil. Koshi affected areas still contain and pester forest, though reclamation is in progress. Small trees such as Babul, Jhaua Harjora etc. and water berries such as Makhana, Ramdana and Motha gass are also found. Sabai grass and munjan also grown in this district. Though the Koshi has distroyed a large number fruit-bearing trees but this region still produces a large quantity of Manges, other common trees are Mahua, Jack fruit, Bancc, Straw Berry, Black berry, Dates, Rose, Rose wood semal, are for timber and lichi, Guava, Lemon, Watermelon, Coconut and Bettle nut are also grown.

The rendation of forests, one reclamation of kans and pater infested waste land and indiscriminate hunting in the part have led to the decline of tiger, panther, Deer, chital, wild bear etc, Nilagai and Khikhir are still found. Jackals, monkey, wolves are also common. Several deadly species of repliles such as cobra, karait and various kinds of lizards are also found.

Jungle crow, house crow, gray horn bill, little brown dove, grey patridge, white breasted water hen, bronze winged jacana, curlew, otint black ebis, glussy ebis, cattle egret, pond heron, pinck headed duck,silli or cotton feal, white fronted goose, large whistling teal, brahminy duck, eastern gray duck are the different varities of birds found in the district.

Land and Pattern

Agriculture is the main occupation of the people of this region. The trubulent Koshi has been controlled considerably and the completion of the Koshi project has helped bringing about change in the cropping pattern. Now in this region jute, Maize are grown in large quantities. Both Bhedai and Aghani paddy are grown , sugar cane cultivation and wheat cultivation has increased. The principal crops grown in this area are paddy, maize, jute, wheat, Barley, Khescari, Moong, Arhar, Meath, Beans, Kalai and sugar cane.Water berry like sorkhi, Singahara and Makhana are also the important money crops of this area. The area also produces Potato, Brinjal, Lady's finger, Tomato, cauli flower, pumpkin cucurbita gourd, Sweet Gourd, Cabbage, Beans etc. Parbal is the main vegetable crop in the flood affected areas. By the side of Koshi river large quantities of palbal are grown. The sandyadira lands produce large number of water melons and cucumber.

Irrigation Facilities

After independence considerable attention has been paid to the provision of irrigation in this areas by means of flood control reasoures as well as irrigation canals. In addition to this open borings, tube well, rahat pups, Bamboo boring are the means of irrigation. Agricultural land of this area is not properly levelled. So it is very difficult to irrigate the major portion of the land. Though the flood has been controlled by the eastern and western embankment, still the seapage from Koshi canals and rivers renders a large tract of neighbouring lands unifit for cultivation.

Forestry

There is no forest in the district but there is plan for planting various types of trees viz.Sisam, Eucalyptes,Gulmohar, Sakhua etc. Along the Koshi canal under the forest extension plan. Forestry has also attracted the people in the direction. People have strated to plant Sesam, Sakhua etc.

Fishery

Fishery is one of the most important occupations of the district. Fishes are sent outside from this area. A good source of money is earned by selling fishes. Thousands of fishermen of the district get employment through this occupation.

Industrialization

Industrially this area is still quite backward. The district had neither adequate resources nor the infrastructure required for industrial development.

However the Bihar state Industrial Development Corporation Ltd, had launched a project to establish a paper factory at Baijnathpur. A wholly state owned subsidiary company named the Bihar paper Mills Ltd, has been formed for the purpose. A number of acilliary industries related to starch grinding,dye,chemicals, mechanical work shops are also likely to be sent up near the paper factory.

In addition to the paper plant, the Bihar state Industrial Development Corporation Ltd is also considering the setting up of another factory for light roofing material in the campus of the paper mill. The plant would be based on the utilization of some locally available raw materials such as rice straw waste paper, raw picking and bamboo.

One private steel re-rolling factory is under construction at patuha. Various types of small scale industries such as candle making, candy manufacturing, soap manufacturing, cake and biscuit factory etc. have also been established in the disrict which give employment to the concerned skilled and unskilled labourers.

The inception of sericulture with the aid and assistance of central silk board and state government angurs well for the farmers of the area.

Language

Hindi, Sanskrit, Maithili, Bhojpuri are spoken in this area. But Maithili is the common language. Even Marwari, Santhal, Bengali, Muslim, Punjabi (who have settled here) can easily express themselves in maithili tongue.

Religion and Caste

This district population consists of Hindu, Muslim, Sikh, Jain, and Christian things in this district has been found that mostly santhals of the district have not embraced christianity. Brahmin, Rajput, Kayasth, Bhumihar,Harijan, Santhal, Yadav, Kurmi, Nai, Mallah, Sonar, Halkhor, Dhanuk, Mushahar, Dom are the main caste of this region.

Communications and other facilities

All the blocks of the district are linked with pucca road to the district head quarter. Saharsa is directly with national high way-purnea. One more road has been completed through Doomri bridge on Koshi. Saharsa is directly connected to Nepal by road. Saharsa district head-quarter is a railway junction, where the trains from forbesganj, Katihar, Bihariganj and Manshi converge and steam off to destinations. One aerodrom is also situated at saharsa district head quarter. As for educational facilities is concerned there are many schools and colleges in this district. But the standard of teaching is not up to mark. Saharsa has got a low power transmission centre for T.V.relay. It has also got microwave facilities.

The Saharsa district is consisting of 40.8% cultivators, 48.39% agricultural laboures, 16.03% S.C.O 40% S.T. Literacy rate of this district is 20.26%.

Bihara

The main area under study (sample village) is 'Bihara' village adjacent to the municipal boundary of Saharsa just 8 K.M. on north and west direction. This village is linked with pucca road. Bihara village is famous because of Kartic purnima fare held every year. About four thousand people assemble here from contiguous villages to worship 'God Kartic' and to witness the fare. This village has one police station, Health centre, Veterinary Hospital, Khadi Bhandar and one Gram panchyat building, one middle school is also situated in this village and another school in situated in Santhali tola (Sautari). Now the village is connected with telephone services.

This village is bounded in the east by Dorma village, in the west by Garaul and Manjhaul village, in the north by patori village and in south by Sihaul village.

The village has remained backward but now is moving towards growth and prosperity. It has the composite structure of caste. The breakup of the more than five thousand adult population is shown on page No 18.

As regards climatic condition, flora and fauna, land use pattern, irrigating facilities, forcestry, weather it is same as it has been discribed about Saharsa district. The cereals, pulses, oil seeds and cash crops produced in the district are common about this village also. The fishes are reared in ponds and found in the rivers and marshes. There is also abundence of crabs and snails which are tastly consumed by the down-trodden. She goat, goat, Hen, Cock, Buffallo, Ox and Hog are domestic pet.

S.No.	Cast	No.
1.	Brahmin	201
2.	Rajput	102
3.	Bhumihar	2031
4.	Kayasth	304
5.	Harijan	501
6.	Santhal	599
7.	Yadav	499
8.	Kurmi	206
9.	Nai(Hajam)	104
10.	Mallah	100
11.	Sonar	101
12.	Muslim	299

There is plenty of mango, jackfruit, sisam, Bamboo palm and Khajur tree in this village. It is pertinent to point here that palm and Khajur trees are the money crop, yielding to pasicaste perennial source of livelihood in the form of 'tody'.

One very important feature regarding land of this village is that some portions of land are well levelled so the agriculturists can easily grow more and more by the new methods of cultivations (Manuring and artificial irrigation)

As per Government documents each family of the village has its own home-stead land based on the Bas-Dih parcha already issued to them.But so far the agricultural land is concerned only 1900 dewellers have their own land, the rest depend either on wages or Bataidari.

As both the majority of landed peasantary and landless people, small, and marginal farmers and agricultural labourers or indirectly depend upon agriculture (land), it is the neucleus of social tension as big land owners are unwilling to part with their surplus land to down-trodden landless. The landless want some share in the land which they till and harvest; tension has been spontaneously generated.

Different socio-economic welfare schemes launched by the Government have only marginlally alleviated the hardship of the weaker sections of the society. The leftist forces championing the cause of down-trodden are arousing new hopes and aspirations for better life. The two opposing poles have established a nucleus of tension in the village. Plarization of haves and Have-nots may be seen in this village in obvious form. Dissatisfaction with economic and social conditions has engendered violence through-out north Bihar.(Stephen P. Huyder: 1985).

Social tension have already erupted in the forms of violent group clashes. Musclc and money powers have temporarily been able to assert their dominance, yet as nucclcus of the tension, social and economic inequality, still exists and is being aggravated as days pass. This social tension is taking ugly shapes and is ventilation it self in many ways. Severe tension and conflict came on the surface on 22nd November 1978 and resulted in loot and arson of huts of ST/SC. 8 people of santhal community were killed.

Bhumihars are the dominant caste because they are very developed and conscious in respect of education and wealth. Some are ex-petty zamindars. At the same time Bhumihar consists of 40% of the total population of the village. But unique thing is that a person from Rajput caste Sri Kumar Singh, was elected Mukhiya of this village. Because he was very much devoted to the common causes of the people and always shares the suffering of the general mass of the poor adivasis and Harijans. At the same time he is related to the politics of leftist force. It is to be quoted here that due to tension Mr. Kumar singh has been killed by some vested interest in 1995 at Saharsa head quarter in the broadday light.

•

3 METHODOLOGY

The scientific study of social problem has been conducted at two different levels. In the first case, the purpose of study is the analysis of facts for giving generalization and for discovering new facts or verifying old facts. The actual aim or objective is the advancement of knowledge and achievement in the academic discoveries. On the other hand the purpose of study is to understand the specific problem which is localised. The analysis of this localised specific problem or it may be confined to the understanding of problem for knowing the existing trends. Thus this type of study is more utiliterian and less academic. The first level of study is decribed as social research while next one is described as social survey.

The present study may help in formulation any generalization or giving a new theme. Hence it is indentical with the principle of research. The first important point in developing methodology or preparing a design is concerned with the fact that the present study is research work.

The following research methods and tools have been employed in carrying out the present research work:

1. Census
2. Sampling
3. Interview
4. Use of schedule
5. Non-Participant observation

Census

The researcher first of all collected the census reports and map of the village. The preparation of map was done by tracing out the boundries, locality and routes. Having completing the mapping business the work of census was undertaken in which the name, Sex, Age and caste of the heads of each family was noted down.

Sampling

The important stage of the research work is concerned with the problem of sampling. The necessity of sampling arises when the universe understudy is very large and analysis of all the units is not possible. The term sample refers to that part of entire universe which retains all the qualities and characteristics of later and is representative part of the whole. Here it will not be out of place to mention that in the present study it was not possible for some research investigator to collect the data from whole rural area of India or from whole rural area of Bihar or from whole Saharsa district. So as per convenience one conflict and tension-prone village,'Bihara'of Saharsa district was selected for data collection. Another point for selecting this village for study is that this village is very conscious in politics and it consists of the composite population of many caste: scheduled tribes Muslim and Haves and Have nots.

SL.NO.	Name of the Caste (franchise)	Total Population	Total household head
1	2	3	4
1.	Brahmin	201	21
2.	Rajput	102	12
3.	Bhumihar	2031	201
4.	Kayasth	304	40
5.	Yadav	499	72
6.	Kurmi	206	30
7.	Nai	104	16
8.	Mallah	100	19
9.	Sonar	101	18
10.	Mushar (SC)	199	25
11.	Dusadh (SC)	302	47
12.	Santhal (ST)	599	78
13.	Saikh Muslim (FC)	79	12
14.	Saiyed Muslim (FC)	49	8
15.	Dhunia Muslim(BC)	71	6
16.	Kujra Muslim (BC)	69	7
17.	Bakho Muslim (BC)	31	3
	Total	**5047**	**615**

For selecting the unit for study again sampling method was applied. Social scientists have developed a number of techniques for selection of sample. The applicability of the particular technique depends upon the nature of the problem, nature of the universe, nature of the units to be selected, purpose of study, funds and time at disposal. Every researcher decides for himself the applicability of the paricular sampling technique in his study. Hence the present researcher was also required to decide as to what technique he should apply in the selection of units from universe on the basis of stratificed random sampling.

It has been stated above on the basis of census each and every house hold head was noted. Whole house hold head was stratified on caste basis. Mentioned below is the population figure of franchise and household head on the basis of caste:

Thus the total adult population of the village under study is 5047 and total house hold head of the village under study is 615. In selecting the unit from the universe it was kept in mind to select the unit proportionately as per their number but in some cases due to heterogeniety some indegenous number was also taken. But 3:1 proportinate sample was selected from the universe. The number of units selected was as follows:

SL.NO.	Caste No.of	Sample Selected
1.	Brahmin	07
2.	Rajput	04
3.	Bhumihar	66
4.	Kayasth	12
5.	Yadav	24
6.	Kurmi	10
7.	Mallah	06
8.	Sonar	06
9.	Mushhar	08
10.	Dusadh	15
11.	Santhal	25
12.	Saikh	04
13.	Saiyed	03
14.	Dhunia	02
15.	Kunjra	02
16.	Bakho	03
	Total	**200**

After deciding the number of units to be selected from caste, the units were selected on the principle of lottery method of random sampling. In this way 200 house hold heads were selected for collecting information. After taking a sample from the universe the researcher was faced with the problem of deciding the technique to be applied for data collection.

Interview

In this study it was decided to apply the technique of structured interview for collecting information from the respondents. It means that the list of questions related to the research work was prepared and on the basis of those set of questions 200 respondents were asked to volunteer their answers. As structured interview is convenient in Tabulation work so in this present research structured interview method has been used for data collection.

Schedule

It has been discussed that the technique of structured interview has been used for collecting information from the respondents. Hence it will not be out of place to mention that schedule is used as to tool for collection responses in structured interview method. In the present study schedule was prepared related to problem concern by the investigator.

Non-participant Observation

In some cases like social relationship, material object possessed by the respondent and other activities were observed through non-patricipant observation.

Difficulties in Data collection

Present researcher collected informations in the systematic manner but at certain stages it was felt that the task of data collection was too difficult to be completed easily. But patience and skillful approach the task of data collection was completed.

The main problem faced by the resercher was to make the respondent agree to answer. While a few of them came forward to answer questions unhesitatingly, majority of them appeared to be unwilling to participate in the interview. Since the co-operation of one and all was vitally essential for the research, the unwilling one had to be persuaded individually to answer the question listed in the schedule. An at long last, the researcher succeeded in eliciting satisfactory response from each one of them. Most of the respondents, however, agreed to answer questions related to their, income, materials possession and land holding. It was only on the assurance that their figures would be ket a secret that they gave out delailed information.

Another difficulty that stood in the way of data collection originated from the doubts and apprehensions of the respondents in respect of the aims and objects of the enquiries by the researchers. Quite a good number of them mistook the agents deputed by the government.They seemed to be in suspicion that their responses might put them to trouble in days to come.

The researcher had to face yet another difficulty in respect of explaining to be respondents the same set of questions repeately and that also in different ways. All this had to be done so as to draw out from them all information relevent to schedule. It was thus that the data collection could be made possible.

The researchers had to face some difficulties in explaining to respondents some of the questions more than once indifferent ways. Some of the respondents were either illiterate or just literate so they were unable to understand the questions in one time. Each and every question of the schedule had to be explained in Maithili Language to many respondents because Maithili is the regional language of the area concerned. The present investigator also belonged to Maithili speaking area hence in these cases language proved no barrier to them. But related to Santhal respondent reseracher had to face difficulty of language. One literate interpretor was chosen from among Santhal, to help in translating the question in Santhali.

4 AN ACCOUNT OF THE SAMPLE UNDER STUDY

As it has been stated in the Methodology chapter that two hundred repondents have been selected for the study. The responses were recored on the schedule and with help of generous responses, the problem could be analysed. For this purpose the classification of data collection was done and the tables were framed.

It has already been stated that only two hundred respondents were selected from different families were of different age groups, sex groups and castes. Moreover, they differed from each other in respect of income, qualifications and social status. The sample, thus, understudy is not a homogeneous group, rather it is characterised by heterogenity and differentiation of respondents.

Table -1

Composition of the respondents on the basis of occupation.

Sl.No.	Occupation	No.of Respondents (In percentage)	
		Main	Subsidiary
1.	Labour	35	0
2.	Caste occupation	06	0
3.	Business	01	0
4.	Service	16	0
5.	Independent Occupation	02	0
6.	Agriculture	40	26
	Total:	**100**	**26**

It appears from the table that respondents belonged to different occupational groups. The occupation to which the respondents belonged arc thc oocupation of labour, caste occupation, Business, Service, Independent occupation and agriculture. The table further shows some of the occupation are primary occupations for some respondents, while some other occupations have been adopted as secondary means of livelihood Moreover, only 26% of the total number of the respondents have subsidiary occupation. It means that only one fourth respondents from total number of respondents have subsidiary occupation. The table further shows that only agriculture has been shown the subsidiary occupation. No respondent has shown his subsidiary livelihood as labour, caste occupation, Business, Service or independent occupation. As regards primary occupation the maximum number of the respondent are found to have adopted agriculture and labour occupation as the primary means of livelihood. As 35% of the respondents are engaged in labour occupation. Morever, 40% of the total number of the respondents have adopted agriculture as their main source of livelihood. Table further indicates that 6% of the respondents are those for whom caste occupation is the means of subsistence. It is generally stated that in caste system caste occupations are losing its importance but the findings of this table under analysis present that caste occupations have not lost their importance. In rural areas caste occupation or jagmani system is still prevailing. In the area under stydy Nai, Brahmin, Bhuniya, Kujara and Sonar are still engaged in caste occupation. Table further shows that 1% respondents are engaged in business 2% of the total number of respondents are engaged in independent occupation. The independent occupation was homeopathy practice and 2 persons were contractors. Table further shows that 16% of the total No.of the respondents are engaged in service. Literacy rate is low so the table indicate that in area under study the number of labourer and agriculturist respondents are high.

Table - 2

Composition of the respondents on the basis of marital status.

Sl. No.	Marital Status	No. of respondents in percentage.
1.	Married	96
2.	Unmarried	02
3.	Widow	00
4.	Widower	02
5.	Divorce	00
	Total	**100**

It appears from the table that all the respondents belonged to three different categories. No respondent is widow or divorced. Moreover, 96% of the total number of the respondents are found to be married. It means that majority of the respondents are those whose life pârtners are still alive and they are enjoying satisfied married life. On the contrary 2% of the total number of the respondents are widower. Their wives have lost their lives and they are leading their lives without wives. In the same way those respondents who are unmarried are 2% of the total number of the respondents. It will not be out of place to mention that responses were collected from the household head. In 2% of the families unmarried youth were house hold heads hence they were included in the sample. The unmarried youth who were selected as the respondents are graduate. They are aspiring for government jobs but now they are engaged in agriculture work. Due to the death of their fathers they are compelled to carry on their families on their shoulders. So as household head they were included in the sample.

Table No- 3

Composition of the respondents on the basis of sex.

Sl.No.	Sex.	No. of the respondents in precentage.
1.	Male	100
2.	Female	00
	Total	**100**

It appears from the above table that 100% of the total number of the respondents belonged to a particular sex. i.e.Male. It has already been pointed out in the chapter dealing with the Methodology that responses were collected from house hold heads hence only house hold heads were selected as sample. The findings of this table help in drwing this inference that 100% of the respondents belonged to partiarchal families and they rule over the female members of their families. At the same time area under study is rural area so till now dominance of women in families always avoided. So no female members could be included in the sample.

It appears from the table there are 17 castes in the village under study. Maximum number of caste respondents belong to Bhumihar caste i.e. 33% of total number of the respondents, minimum number of the respondents have been collected from Bakho caste only. 0.5% low muslim caste. Caste wise break up of percentage of respondents is as follows:-

Brahmin 3.5 % Rajput 2%. Kayasth 6%. Yadav 12%, Kurmi 5%, Nai 2.5%, Mallah 3%, Sonar 3%, Dusadh 7.5%, Santhal 12.5%, Saikh 2%, Saiyed 1.5%. Dhuniyal 1%, Kujra 1%. If we divide the whole respondents on high caste group, backward caste group and low caste group we find that 44.5% respondent belong to high Hindu caste group, 3.5% belong to high muslim caste group.48% of the total number of respondents belong to high caste group, 25.5% belong to backward muslim caste group. 28% of the total number of the respondent belongs to backward caste group. And rest 24% of the respondent belongs to low caste group. i.c. Harijan and adivasi (S.C./S.T.). It will not be out of point to discuss here that in muslim society there is no caste classification but government has classified the muslim community in backward and forward muslim. Accepting govt. classification of muslim caste, saiyeds and sheikhs have been placed in forward and rest in back-ward group. In Hindu caste classification governement classification has been kept in mind.

Table - 4

Composition of the respondents on the basis of caste.

Sl. No.	Caste	No of respondents in percentage.
1.	Brahimin	03.5
2.	Rajput	02
3.	Bhumihar	33
4.	Kayasth	06
5.	Yadav	12
6.	Kurmi	05
7.	Nai	02.5
8.	Mallah	03
9.	Sonar	03
10.	Mushhar	04
11.	Dushadh	07.5
12.	Santhal	12.5
13.	Saikh	02
14.	Saiyed	01.5
15.	Dhuniya	01
16.	Kujra	01
17.	Bakho	05
	Total	**100%**

Table No:-5

Composition of the respondents on the basis of religion.

SL.NO.	Religion	No.of respondents in percentage.
1.	Hinduism	94
2.	Islam	06
3.	Sikh	00
4.	Christian	00
	Total	**100**

It appears from the table that the respondents belong to only two religious groups. The table indicates that 94% of the respondents believe in Hinduism and only 6% of the respondents believe in Islam. Though all santhal had answered that they are Hindu but they differ in their mode of worship from traditional Hindu.

Table -6

Composition of the respondents on the basis of age group

Sl.No.	Age group.	No.of the respondents in percentage.
1.	Up to 20 Years	00
2.	21 Years to 30 Years	20
3.	31 Years to 40 Years	34
4.	41 Years to 50 Years	16
5.	51 Years to 60 Years	20
6.	Above 60 Years	10
	Total	**100**

It appears from the table that respondents belong to 5 age groups. The table further shows that no respondent is below 21 years of age. The second age group i.e. the age group of 21 to 30 years is respresented by 20% of the respondent. Moreover, 34% of the respondents belong to 31 to 40 Years age group. The age group of 41 to 50 Years and 51 to 60 Years are represented by 16% and 20% of the respondents respectively. Those respondents who are above 60 Years of age consitute 10% of the total number of the respondents. Thus, It appears that in sample young, grown up and old persons have been included.The respondents up to 30 Years, grown up and old persons have been included.The respondents up 30 Years of age may be regarded as young, they constitute 20% of the respondents.The respondents in the age group of 31-50 Years may be termed as grown up. This age group is represented by 50% of the total number of the respondents. Those who are above 50 Years of age treated as old constitute 30% of the total number of the respondents.When we grouped those age group in another 3 groups we find 20% are up to 30 Years 50% are 31 Years to 50 Years, 30% are more than 51 Years.

It appears from the above table 55% of the respondents belong to illiterate group, 10% of the respondents can read only. 4% of the respondents can read and write and have education up to primary level respectively, 8% of the respondents have got the education of high school, 10% are of that type of resondents who are not graduate but have received the education of college. 1% of the respondents have got the Homeopathy diploma certificate, 4% are graduate and 4% post-graduate. Though adult education programme has been launched in this village but the literacy rate has not improved, only 14% of the respondents feel that mass lieracy programme i.e. adult education programme has encouraged them so they can read and write only.

Table -7

Composition of the respondents on the basis of lieracy.

Sl.No.	Level of Literacy	No.of respondents in percentage.
1	2	3
1.	Illiterate	55
2.	Can read only	10
3.	Can read and write	04
4.	Primary	04
5.	Middle	00
6.	High school	08
7.	College but not graduate	10
8.	Graduate	04
9.	Post Graduate	04
10.	Ph.D.	00
11.	Technical	00
12.	Any other	01
	Total	**100**

Table No.8

Composition of the respondents on the basis of mother tongue.

Sl. No.	Mother tongue	No.of the respondents in percentage.
1.	Maithli	79.5
2.	Hindi	02
3.	Bhojpuri	00
4.	Urdu	06
5.	Santhali	12.5
	Total	**100**

It appears from the table that the respondents belong to three mother tongue groups in varying degree. Minimum number of respondents are those whose mother tongue is Hindi. The person who told his mother tongue is Hindi are in government jobs 6% of the total number of the respondents told that their mother tongue is Urdu. All the respondents of the Muslim community told that their mother tongue is Urdu but at the time of congregation they were talking in regional language, Maithili. The Maximum percentage i.e. 79.5% are in favour of Maithili as their mother tongue. But 12.5% of the total number of the respondents answered that their mother tongue is Santhali.

Table - 9

Composition of the respondents on the basis of types of house in which they live.

Sl. No.	Types of houses	No.of respondents percentage.
1.	Pucca	15
2.	Kachcha	55
3.	Mixed	10
4.	Hut	20
	Total	**100**

It appears from the table that the respondents live in four types of houses mentioned in the table. 15% respondents reside in pucca house, while 10% respondents reside in mixed house that made of bricks and tiled structure (Khapra). 20% of the respondents live in Huts. Most of the respondents i.e. 55% of the respondents live in Kuchcha house. It may be concluded from this table that only 15% of the respondents live in pucca building. It means that 85% of the respondents are living in mixed or Kachcha or huts. The condition of the houses is indicative of the economic status of the respondents.

Table - 10

Composition of the respondents on the basis of houses in which the respondents.

Sl.No.	Nature of house	No.of the respondent in percentage.
1.	Own house	89
2.	House on rent	01
3.	House of relative	10
	Total	**100**

It appears from the table that 89% of the respondent do have the houses of their own in the village under study. These respondents who are not in possession of the houses of their own in village under study and live in rented building constitute only 1% of the total number of respondents. A glance at the table shown that 10% of the respondents live in the houses of their relatives. They have come here in search of the means of livelihood and are residing in the huts of their in-laws.

Table No. 11

Composition of the respondents who have own land for cultivation.

Sl.No.	Nature of the respondents	No.of respondent in percentage.
1.	Have land for cultivation	40
2.	Have no land for cultivation	60
	Total	**100**

It appears from the table that 40% of the respondents have own land for cultivation and 60% of terespondents have no land for cultivation, their means of livelihood is either laboure or Bataidari of land. It shows that the of majority of the respondents economic condition is not good as far as income from land is concerned.

Table No. 12

Possession of land by respondents.

Sl.No.	Possession of land in acres	No.of respondents in percentage
1.	Less than 1 acre	20
2.	1 acre to 5 acres	02
3.	6 acres to 10 acres	04
4.	11 acres to 20 acres	00
5.	21 acres to 30 acres	04
6.	More than 31 acres	10
	Total	**40**

The respondents who replied that they have land for cultivation they were again asked how many acres of land they have for cultivation. This table shows that 20% of the respondents are of those who have land for cultivation but less than one acre 2% of the respondents are of those category who have own land for cultivation upto 5 acres. 4% of the respondents are of those category who have own land for cultivation up to 10 acres and up to 30 acres respectively. 10% of the respondents are of those category who have own land for cultivation more than 30 acres. Those category who have own land for cultivation more than 30 acres. 22% of the respondents belong yo marginal farmers.

On the basis of this table land peasantry for the sake of convenience may be categorised in to three classes:

1. 22% are marginal and small farmers.
2. 8% of farmers whose lands do not exceed the ceilinglimits.
3. 10% big farmers with land exceeding ceiling limits.

Table 13

Composition of the respondents on the basis of monthly income.

Sl.No.	Monthly income	No.of respondents in percentage.
1.	Up. Rs. 50 only	0
2.	Rs. 51 to Rs. 100	0
3.	Rs. 101 to Rs. 300	0
4.	Rs. 301 to Rs.500	0
5.	Rs. 501 to Rs. 700	24
6.	Rs. 701 to Rs. 900	50
7.	Rs. 901 to Rs. 1100	00
8.	More than Rs. 1100	26
	Total	**100**

It appears from the table that respondents belong to only three income groups 24% of the respondents are in the monthly income group ganging between Rs. 501 to Rs. 700. The second group of the respondents which constitute 50% of the respondents have monthly income of Rs. 701 to Rs. 900. And third group consisting of 26% of the respondents have monthly earning above Rs. 1100.

It appears from the table that 75% of the total number of respondents have shown that they are related to some organization 15% of the respondents belong to religious organization. 51% of the respondents have told that they belong to any political organization i.e. communist party, congress party, Janta Dal or any other politcal party. 4% of the respondents told that they are related to academic organization i.e. teacher's organization 1% of the respondents answered that they are related to occupational organization. 4% of the respondents answered that they are related to cultural organization. Thus table indicates that enough political consciousness is persisting in the area under study so the majority of the respondents are related to political organization.

Table No. 14

Composition of the respondents on the basis of their relation with different organizations.

Sl.No.	Name of the organization	No.of respondents	Disignation	Member
1.	Voluntary organization	0	0	0
2.	Religious organization	30	28	2
3.	Political organization	102	98	4
4.	Academic organization	8	8	0
5.	Occupational organization	2	2	0
6.	Cultural organization	8	8	0
	Total	**150**	**144**	**6**

Table No. 15

Composition of the respondents on the basis of habit of reading news papers and magzines.

Sl.No.	Habits of reading News paper and magazines	No.of respondents reading news paper	Magazines.
1.	Regularly	10	2
2.	Occasionally	11	10
3.	Rarely	10	10
4.	Do not read	169	178
	Total	**200**	**200**

It appears from the above table that 5% of the respondents read news papers regularly 5.2% of the respondents read news paper occasionally. whereas 84.5% of the respondents don't read news paper at all. As regards magazines 5% of the respondents read magazines in very low.

Table No. 16

Composition of the respondents on thebasis of material objects in possession.

Sl.No.	Materialobjectsin possession	No.of respondents in percentage
1.	Cycle	25
2.	Watch	40
3.	Sofa	05
4.	Scooter/Motor Cycle	05
5.	Refrigerator	00
6.	T.V.	05
7	Radio/Transistor	26
8.	Pressure Cooker	10
9.	Threasser	03
10.	Pumping Set	10
11.	Gasoven	05
12.	Tape recorder	08
13.	Record Player	00
14.	Air cooler	00
15.	Gun/Pistol	02
16.	Tractor	02
17.	Motor Car	00

It appears from the table that 25% of the respondents possess cycle, 40% of the respondents have Watch, 5% of the respondents have Sofa, 5% of the respondents have T.V, 26% of the respondents have pressure Cooker, 3% of the respondents have Thresser,19% of the respondents have pumping sets, 5% of the respondents have Gas-overn,8% of the respondents have Tape recorder,2% of the respondents have Tractor. The table shows that only few of the respondents are of those category whose standard of living is good. Though Governement agencies have distributed jumping set among Harijans of the area concerned but now they have no pumping set.They have sold those pumping sets at low prices to the economically sound persons. More over this table shows that generally the luxurious goods are not possessed by most of the respondents.

5 ECONOMY AND TENSION

Social thinker late Dr. Narmadeshwar Prasad has rightly remarked "A Society is tension free only when it is closed or an immobile society. A developing society function on the basis of resistances and tensions.Tensions exist because of an inherent clash between a tradition and modernity. Quite often, they are legacies of the pasts, accentuated by economic growth often, in the process of development, some of the tensions are fully or partially resolved. There is a dichotomous relationship between the forces of stability and conservation and the former of change and expansion. The developing society faces these problems rather acutely. (Prasad:1970:108).

India is a developing country and it may not be treated as an exceptional case with regard to the existence of tension. Paricularly rural scene in India is basically scene of conflict, and tension overt and covert. It is this tension that must be understood before a solution can be offered.

A variety of the theories of tension or violence has been developed in the social sciences. We will therefore turn to those theories in order to see if they can help in explicating rural tension in India.

THEORIES OF TENSION

(1) Marxist Theory

German philosopher, Karl Marx, looked upon the economy as the most important factor to create any problem specially, the problem of tension. Marx asserted that economic factors are not only responsible for creating different problems rather they are also responsible for determining the general character of social life. In his own words, the mode of producation in material life determines the general character of social, political and spiritual process of life".(Marx:1956:11-12) It may be assumed that there are highly differentiated interest groups. All evidences of history point to class as the basis of action and consciousness. The group, whether nation, tribe,class and the myth which it engenders has been comparably the most potent factor in mobilizing men's allegance. The actual community to which men belong is that with which they indentify themselves, often to the point of dying for it. For it unlike class is where life is lived in association with other. (Marx:1956 :11-12). After formation of group one supports the old norms of relationship and the other fights for the new mode, consequently class struggle develops. The problems of struggle has been a universal problem through out the history of class struggle in the words of Marx" The history of all hither to existing society is the history of class struggle.(Marx:1956:12-13). Marx has further pointed out that freeman and slave, partisan and peasant, lord and serf, Guildmaster and journeyman, oppressor and oppressed stood in constant opposition to one another carried on an uniterupted, now, hidden, now open fight, a fight that each time ended either in a revolutionary reconstitution of society at large or in the common ruin of the contesting classes. He has also pointed out that the modern Bourgeois society that has sprouted from the ruins of feudal society has not done away with class antagonism. It has not established new classes, new conditions of oppressions and new forms of struggle in the place of the old ones.

The primary source of contradiction of human society is its division into classes i.e.exploiters and the exploited. Exploitation in Marx has a specific connotation. By exploitation is meant the expropriation of the surplus value i.e. the profit which is noting but the surplus power of the labour. How does this surplus accrue to the owner?

Marx is specific on this aspect of this theory. They surplus i.e. the profit, is the end product of the labour expended on producing the product minus the actual payment received by the labour in the form of wages. The greater is the surplus i.e. the profit the more intensive in the exploitation. In fact Marx termed this payment as means of subsistence but differently, the subsistence means is the wage which is just enough to maintain the labour.

In the Marxian scheme therefore, a confrontation emerges between the owers and the workers i.e.the capital and labour. It is confrontation between the exploiters and exploited perpetually locked in struggle, some times latent and some time manifest.Tension therfore, is the result of exploitation.Exploitation is the expropriation of surplus value produced by the labour. And the expropriation of surplus gains gives rise to alienation.Therefore, the greater the alienation, the greater is the probability to tension. However manifestation of the tension as conflict or violence can be resorted to from both sides-exploiters and the exploited depending on the specific contexts. One every critical element in the

Marxian formulation is the economic factor and that is the material basis.

(ii) Structural Functional Theory

The structural functional theory starts not with the division of society into classes but with the total social system. According to the theory, society is looked upon as an organism with various parts (Sub-structure) in compatible with each other. These sub-structures are values norms role and collectivity(sub-group). So long as these are broadly held in compatible relationship, society is stable, in a homeostatic state.

However, society according to the theory is never in perfect harmony. There are always present one or other kinds of strains that constantly press upon the system. These strains may be expressed in several way. They may either be generated internally or externally, leading to changes in the hither-to prevalent value, norms, role and sub-group (collectivity) structures. How conceptions of values may arise, new roles may replace the old ones and sub-groups in society may either question their own status or acquire new roles.

Thus when such kinds of strains are produced upon the system, it moves towards adaptation with them. The system therefore may adapt to the strains so produced by the existing institutionalised mechanisms, like the law courts, legislatures, collective bargaining, political parties; or it might innovate new mechanism within its own frame work.

However, when strains become too over-whelming to reckon with, society seeks measures other than institutionalised or innovated mechanisms;these mechanisms are sought out-side the framework of the system. And one of these may be conflict,violence and tension.

Underlying the structural functional theory is a belief that society is in a steady state. It returns to this state, once disturbance caused by strains are resolved.The steady state may be restored at the same level or it might move to another level.

But when the systems mechanisms fail and prove ineffective to cope up with the strains generated either internally or externally, a period of unsteadiness, disequilibrium occurs.This is the period when society is passing through a phase of rapid social changes. Conflict, violence and tension, therefore, is the indicators of such unsteadiness or disequilibrium.

(iii) Relative Deprivation Theory

Relative deprivation theory is a psychological theory related to conflict, violence and tension. Scholars like Gurr, Fierabends and Nezvold and Devices have made notable contribution to elaborating explaining and developing the theory in all its niceties and details.(Fierabland:1972)

In viewing tension economic deprivation of one sort or another has been a recurring theme.This deprivation is equated with inequality, the reasons for tension are attributed to the persistence of inequality in society.Aristotle held that the "cause of sedition is always to be found in inequality."(Hautington:1969:50). Marx's own formulation was predicted upon economic inequality between classes.

According to relative deprivation theory deprivation leads to tension and conflict. It accurs because there is gap between expectation and achivevement. The difinition provided by Gurr is relevant to quote here."The neccessary precondition for violent civil conflict is relative deprivation, defined as actors" perception for discrepancy between their value expectations and their environment's apparent value capabilities.Value expectations are the goods and conditions of life to which people believe they are justifiably entitled. The reference of value capabilities is to be found largely in the social and physical environments. They are the conditions that determine people's perceived chances of getting or keeping the value they legitimately expect to attain. (Gurr:1970:319).

In the definition, given above, there are three critical variables involved. First relative deprivation exists when a certain value is expected but its actual achievement is difficult to attain. Second, it is not enough that a gap between expectation and achievement should exist. It is also necessary that the actors involved should perecive it, should be conscious of it. And lastly value expectation is always with reference to some social collectivities or environment's dimensions. The reference may be groups or goods and service.

Relative deprivation may acquire three forms. Runcimen has classified them under three heads. These are derived from Max Weber's concept of class, status and power. (Runcimen:1966:72).

In so far as class is concerned, relative deprivation may be correlated with income, occupational opportunities, working conditions, etc.

However, in regard to status, relative deprivation may be felt in terms of social estimation, Social prestige, race, age and sex. The last of the variables, that is power, with reference to Relative Deprivation, is experienced when individuals or groups find themselves incapable of exercising their will independent of the opposition of others. (Wilson:1973:72).

In the ultimate analysis it may be said the whole thing of tension, conflict or violence is related to the structural dimension of the social system. It relates to the factors scored under class, status and power discrepancy. It may be articulated in several ways. A group may feel relatively deprived, if it realises that it is entitled to get a certain value which it is deprived of presently. But differently, the discrepancy between the expected and the actual gives a sense of deprivation. Second group might feel that a value it has so far been entitled to is either declining, threatened or challenged. Such a perception may also cause a sense of relative deprivation. In substance the Relative Deprivation culminates in tension.

Tension reflects a state of distrubed homeostasis. In the present book it has been tried to scrutinize the contemporary reality of rural social tension which has assumed newer facets. Shapes and dimensions in present set up. In India, to understand the shapes and dimensions of tensions studies have been under taken by sociologist. After the sixties attention has been given towards specialised social tension areas such as rural stratification, peasant unrest, agrarian movements, agrarian struggles, agrarian conflict, agrarian tensions etc.

In the explanations available to us about rural tension, invariably the character and contours of these analysis have been bio-focal in nature. In these studies the attempt has been made to focus attention on the reality that in rural tension.There is an aggressor and a victim who is poor on all the counts. These explanations continue to have their relavance and efficacy but would only partially explain the total reality of rural tensions (Prasad:1975). To explain rural tensions in the contemporary era and to describe their total gamut certain other dimensions need to be encompassed. Achievements in the sphere of technology, economic growth, educational attainment, legislative safe-guards, awareness and other sources of information are addding to the reality of rural life. (Hiramani:1977 and Laxminarayan:1976). In the backdrop of these realities, the rural people are expected to play multiple roles and confront varied situations.

The agrarian system as it evolved during the British regime in India was based either on the Zamindari or the Ryotwari type of land settlements, the Mahalwari system was yet another variety of land system but it closely resembled the zamindari pattern of settlement, and the difference was mainly in the mode of revenue assessment on the land.

All the three systems generated more or less a similar agrarian class structure in the villages. The zamindary system had the zamindars, tenants and agricultural labourers as the main agrarian classes. The Ryotwari system consisted of two types of peasants: the ryot landlord and the ryot peasants.In fact, the landlordism which was rural in the zamindari areas had a defacto existence in the ryotwari areas. The agrarian class structure, every where in India, had a feudalist character; the zamindars were tax gather and non-cultivating owners of land, the tenants were the real cultivators, often without security of land tenure and the agricultural labourers in most parts of the country had status of bonds men and hereditary attached labourers. With the support of the British colonial power this highly exploitative system continued to persist despite frequent peasant unrests and movements.

The challenge to the feudal class structure emerged with the rise of the nationalist movement. Not only was a radical agrarian ideology accepted (Sec.P.C.Joshi,1971:H.D. Malaviya 1955:U.P.Zamindari, Abolition committee Report, 1948) but the national leadership activity undertook the cause of the exploited peasantry and led to kisan movements in various parts of the country. Following independence, therefore, the land reforms were introduced in most states and a beginning was made for transformations in the agrarian class structure. Most sociological studies of the agrarian structure refer to these processes of social change.

Before we take up the substantive problem as highlighted by sociological studies on agrarian class stratification it may be useful to discuss briefly the methodology implicit in most such studies about the notion of agrarian class. As we mentioned above, most formulations of class are either 'interactional' or 'attributional' or mixed ones. The interactional formulations in most cases have a Marxist theoretical frame. Daniel Tharner uses the term 'Malik' agrarian classes (D.Thorner:1956); bourgeois i.e.,'Capitalist type landowners' richpeasant landless or land poor'peasantry and agricultural labourers are the class categories mentioned by Kotovsky (G.Kotovsky,1964) in his analysis of agrarian classes in India. Gadgil mentions two important classes in the country side, the substatial landlord and money lander' who according to him dominate over the rural economic system and exploit the 'Cultivators'. An important feature of all these class categories in their emphasis on the processes of class interaction dependence independence and conflict. In some cases, especially in orthodox Marxist formulation, these categories also inherit a whole set of implicit prepositions about the future course of change or revolution, but most other formulations do not have such implicit assumptions. Conceputally, most of these categorises are not nominalistic that they are a name) but imply a set of propositions. To this extent these can be distinguished from the attributional sets of class categories used by other social scientists.

The attributional class categorise used for the analysis of agrarian classes in India are of two types: first, those that use households or holdings as unit for classification, and secondly, those where regions, states or size of holdings etc.are bases for classification. Most classifications used from the Census records are of this type (See,S.C.Gupta, 1969, K.Ghose, 1969:S.M.Shah, 1969 and U.Mehta, 1969); the survey type of studies of agrarian problems have also usually followed this classification. Regions or states are used as units for classification Regions or states are used as units of classification of agrarian structure of analyse its bearing upon the regional development and social stratification (See, Report of the Agricultural Labour Enguiry, Rural Manpower and Occupational structure, 1954). Another form is found in the measurement of 'construction ration's of holdings for various regions to demonstrate inequalities in the distribution of land holdings. The concentration ratio ranges from zero to one; it is zero when all holdings are equally distributed in size, and it is one when all holdings are concentrated into one hand only. The mixed method of class categorisation refers to those approaches where the categories of class are arrived at through attributional measures but each stratum also implies a mode of social interaction. Ramkrishna Mukherjee has formulated three rural class categories out of the nine occupational categories (Ramkrishna Mukherjee 1958). The names these as land holders and supervisory farmers, 'self sufficient peasantry' (consisting to the cultivators and artisans), and the group of share-croppers, agricultural labourers, service holders and other. These, according to him, roughly correspond with the categories of sub infeudatory landlords),'self sufficient peasantry' and the agricultural labourers'. The chief characteristic of Mukherjee's classification in that he works through attributional classification of occupational groups and formulates on the basis three categories of inter actional class strata.

Five agrarian categories in connection with land has been also described by T.K Oomen (1984)(1) Landlords (2) Rich farmers (iii) Middle peasant (IV) Poor peasant (V) landless agricultural labourers.

The significant trends mentioned by the scholars of agrarian class structure in India follwing the International methods are:(1)that there is a wide gap between land reform ideaology projected during the freedom struggle or even thereafter and the actual measures introduced for land reforms. Consequently, socialist transformation in the class structure of the villages has not taken place; (2) this lag could partly be explained by the class character of the Indian political and admisistrative elites, who are resistant to the needed radical reforms; (3) the existing land reforms have initiated a process by which the security of tenure and economic prosperity of the rich peasantry has increased but conditon of the small peasants both inrespect of economic level and tenurial stability has deteriorated; (4) the feudalistic and customary types of tenancy had declined and it has been replaced by a capitalistic form of lease-labour or wage labour agrarian system; (5) a new class of rich middle stratum of peasantry has come into being and not all them are from among the ex-zamindars; (6) the class inequalities between the top and the bottom levels of the classes have increased rather than decreased; (7) the benefits of land reforms have so far not gone as much to the agricultural workers or even as to ex-zamindars as to the emergent middle peasantry; (8) as a result of these contradictions in the agrarian class structure the tension in the rural social system have increased and are bound to increase further; and finally, that (9) the sociological process deminant in the current class transformations in the villages involved 'Embourgeoisement' of some and 'proletarianzation' of many social strata.

The gap between precept and practice in the land reform ideology in India is said to have resulted from the Indians ruling elite's concern to tread on a 'middle path' between the extreme policies of revolutionary land redistribution on the one hand and providing security of tenure by ending intermediary rights of land and implementing land ceilings, on the other. Soon after independence the intermediary rights in land were abolished and ceilings on land holding were imposed. This created owner cultivators and also capitalist farmers who cultivated through hired labourers. These land reformer policies were of course, elite sponsored (P.C.Joshi,1971) and did not emerge from the strong peasant movements or organised unions as in other countries (W.Ladejinsky 1969) Ladejinsky writes in this context."The peasants themselves, while discontented have not developed a movement, whether in the form of tenant unions like those of Japan before the reforms, or peasant political parties like those of western Europe after the first world war. For the most part the peasants behaved as if any change in their conditon depended upon somebody else. By their apathy they desapproved the reasonable assumption that in an agricultural country a government must have peasant support. The fact is that the national and state legislatures in India do not represent the interests of the peasantry; if they did, reform might have taken a different character altogether. The reality is then even when voting is free the peasantry in Asia is not yet voting its own interest (Wolf Ladejinsky, 1964 quoted in P.C. Joshi,1971).

In this context it is very relevent to write here that the expression of 'land reforms' has a misleading connotation. It is said that land has been polluted and needs purifications. Actually the term means reform of the basic relations between man and land, and between tillers of the land and other benificiaries from the land, tiller interaction with landlords, money lenders and village merchants. In a country where 70% of the population is dependent on land, relations between various categories of people like big farmers, share croppers and agricultural labourers on the one hand, and the nature of their respective control overland on the other, is of paramount importance. Any strategy for increasing agricultural protection cannot overlook these structural question just as rural poverty agricultural backwardness cannot be understood without reference to the agrarian strucure.

Land reforms is a subject of controvercy, both intellectually and plitically. The idea of turning over land and its management to uneducated peasants was seen in the pre-independence period as the road to disaster. Landlords were quick to point out the dire consequences of such a policy peasants will produce only for their own needs, food prices will soar, economic growth would be arrested..yet this position is contradicted by historical experience and the confidence placed in the ability of peasants to rise to the challenge has usually been right. However, the development of this latent human potential requires an appropriate institutional environment.The creation of such an environment is what land reform is all about.

The discrepancy between the ownership and operation of land was regarded as one of the basic maladies of our agrarian structure and one that acted as a built in depressor. It led to not only inefficient utilisation of the way augmenting these resources. Thus in every state, the policy at abolishing all intermediary interests and giving land to the recorded tenants was adopted soon after independence followed by a programme of providing security of tenure to the subtenants in some states. At the same time, the research done on size productivity relationship during the 1960s made it clear that in agriculture, given the same resource facilities, soil content and climate, a small farmer produces more per acre than a large farmer. Since it was no longer necessary to identity viability and efficiency with large holdings, the programme of encouraging co-operative farming died a natural death, it also privided on economic rationale to the policy of imposing a ceiling on land holdings that was taken up by many states in the 1960 and then more vigorously by all the states in the mid 1970s.

Democratization in India has shifted slowly and gradualy the centre of gravity of leadership from the urban politicians to the up and coming rural gentry who could command more votes. Especially, this could easily be found if were to have a look at the pattern of leadership that came to held the reins of power in the state ministries, from highly educated men that comprised the earliest ministries in every state there has been a fail or shif into men with, what is politically emphemistic pragnatic wisdom and earthy common political accumers. Examples are plenty, though the chief ministers in general happen to be men of competence not all the ministers can claim acquaintance with the sophistication necessary for running modern governements, though they may subsequantely learn to chimb the ropers. Industrialization urbanisation, transport and communication house all contributed to the well to do in the village not to confine themselves in their villages but to go to the cities, educate their children in the cities, dabble in stocks and shares and invest in various other ventures that opened up as a result of the developmental processes. In various places the problems that used to cause tensions once upon a time ceased to be sources of tension. Panchyaty raj gave further opportunities to the rural leaders to exercise a need kind of power and wield new kinds influence bureaucracy no were is a grals to be respected but a tool to be wielded rural leadership through matremony and corruption has been able to coopt both the urban middle classes working in the bureaucratic echelons as well as the political leaders at the state levels, if not at the central levels. This alters the dynamics of village politics. There is time for petty village factions except in very remote village. Mediations by common friends who are new leaders both on the political, administrative, legal, business and other fields, are possible and due to the availability of imputs for agriculture, peaceful adjustements among the richer communities have become common.

Negatively speaking the cry for land to the tiller has become a part of the political rhetoric. Telangana's armed revelt more than anything else brought into clear focus the need for urgent land refourm. Humbuging the people with 'Bhoodan' did not cut ice.

Land legislations had to be enacted in accordance with electroal promises. But again those who were incharge of legislating and implementing reforms were those who were to stand to lose by them. It is not the bourgeoisic that was carrying out the democratic revolution, but the unholy alliance of kulak, and the capitalist that has successfully demarcated their boundaries. My purpose here is not to go into the nature of the Indian state, but to show that the land reform does not get implemented because of the power that the feudal elements wield in the state apparatus. The legislations take a great deal of time that the affected elements successfully take all the precaution to see that they would not lose anthing. After the so called legislation are subjected to the long and learned'debates in the assemblies comprising these parview, they are seeded with all sorts of loopholes, provisions, exceptions, so that courts may come to the rescue of the same class to which once again the learned members of the legal profession belong. After withstanding all these trials, if the legislation has to be implemented, then the bureaucracy comes to the rescue of its own class. If there were to be any one among the bureaueracy that takes the legislation seriously and tries to implements to reform, the political leader who waxed eloquent about the need for land reformsees to it that the over enthusiasm of the officer is quietly curbed by his transfer.

This state is not a soft State as Gunner Myrdal wants us to believe and has successfully sold the idea among the west of or worshiping intellectual. It is soft on the black marketeers, landlords criminals, sons and son-in-low of men in authority, but if is a very hard, crual, vindicative and efficiently powerful state against poorest sections. Take for example, the ruthlessness with which the pride of our democracy, Nehru dealt with the Telangana agitation for the just rights of the poor peasantry'. Also the way Naxalite prisiners and dealt with does not indicate any softness on the part of the Myrdalian state. The benami transaction, the fictitious divorces by the virtuous 'Hindu' wives for the sake of safe guarding property are all too well known to need any further elaboration.

From the time the land reform was being talked about to this dang, the following table shows the land distributed as against the land that was to be distributed.

First of all, these official figures themselves are not dependable. There are large ownership holdings. There is a large surplus from these holdings. Raj Krishna Report on land Reform mentions that there are more than 2,000 writ petitions pending as 30th June, 1978, concerning land legislations.

Table

SL.NO.	State	Declared Surplus	Actual Distribution
1.	Anddra Pradesh	16,338,65 acres	1,14,493 acres
2.	Assam	5,60,424 acres	46,992 "
3.	Bihar	2,33,383 acres	22,510 "
4.	Gujarat	52,031 acres	40,000 "
5.	Karnataka	1,23,095 acres	9,092 "
6.	Kerala	1,18,737 acres	12,730 "
7.	Madhya Pradesh	33,88,443 acres	60,420 "
8.	Maharashtra	3,52,943 acres	23,501 "
9.	Orissa	1,26,332 acres	5,740 "
10.	Punjab	28,716 acres	303 "
11.	Rajasthan	2,51,736 acres	1,911 "
12.	Uttar Pradesh	2,74,077 acres	61,564 "
13.	West Bangal	1,11,850 acres	1,257 "

(Ministry of Agriculture, GDI)

Again the landlord being the money lender is another well known phenomenon. This condition results in semifeudalism because the landlord does not insist an full clearance of the debt but instead is able to get various unequal benefits like forced labour on his fields and advantageous term for eare etc. The dependence on landlort thus grous interminably and this bond between the labourer and the landlord gives the letter enormous political power. Since most of these labourers are externally in this grip.If there were to be alternate source at employment or an easy way of abtaining loans from governmental soucrces without paying interest, that this bondage can be broken, but the semi-feudal elements that are at the helms of state power will not provide on alterative source of income that would make the agricultural labourer a free proletariat who can sell his labour power to any one of his choice.One is not sure if the Soviet Scholar G.Kotovsky (1964) is right when he said that the post land reform era has recuced the semi feudal exploitation of the peasentry. In fact in the rural areas are any indication of this these falls flat. Most of the peasant uprisings and the agricultural labour unrest followed by violent and fierce reprisals by the landlord have taken place even after the so called land-legislations, to date, they have not abated. The fake implementation of land reform, has further differentiated the rural poor and the caste system has added to the confusion by not permitting the telling of the class struggle in the rural areas. This needs a further explanation.

Among the poorer sections are the peasent who with a small holding perhaps makes a bare sustinance by himself,and all his family members working on the field, a still smaller peasant who may have a ribbon of a holding put ekes out by working on the land of others, another who may have no land at all but works as a tenant,each year praying to god and the landlord that his lease deed he remended and finally, the landless labourer who totally depends from day to day on wages from the landlord. These may be semi-proletariat in the sense that owing to the reduction as bonded labour by virtue of the recoverring deft, they are tied to the master's land for the impossible task of discharging the loan. There are also other proletariat task of who keep moving from one farm to another for their pickings and migrate to the towns and cities during off seasons to earn as urban labourers by pulling rickeshaws or in building sites, and so on. There may be slight variations in the patterns from region to region.

There has been a history of peasant moment in the country and in a number of places there have been revolts of the peasantry as well against the exploitation at the fendal landlords. Mobilisation of the peasantry for national struggle and the consequent formation of kisan organisation led to the creation of the rudiments of class consciousness among the peasantry. Same times they were described as communal agitations as happened in the case of Moplah revolt. It has also been agrued that is some cases the caste has acted as a rallying force for the peasantry.

The consciousness created by the national movement and the peasent movement and more importantly by the communist movement to some extent has been able to mobilise the peasentry strike some fear in the minds of the feudal elements that they cannot have it their way always. The movements have started penetrating deeper into the landless poor whose major composition is sechduled castes. There action, because of the vide despersal of agricultural labour and the non continuius nature of their employment but the fact that there is a stir among them, that there is come inchoate defance among them is some thing that is to be credited to the communist parties. There have been agriculture labour unions in Andhra pradesh, for instance, that put up the joint demand for better wages and did conduct some struggle but due to some of the inherent weaknessses , there movements did not gain much, still these areas are better than places like U.P. and Bihar where the communists had not penetrated deeply. The rudiments of consciousness among the traditionally down troden has caused a great deal of unrest and distrubance.

Telangana, Naxalbari, Kilvenamani in Tajore in 1969. Chandwa Rupaspur in Bihar in 1971, in Cuddappah, A.P.,etc.are all the manifestations of the wrath and intense hatred of thc landlord communitics towards the agricultural labour which also happened to be scheduled caste.There attacks have been fierce striking and inhuman. For example, raping is done in order to fiercely assert and demonstrate the power at the landed classes then just to satisfy the lust raping of old woman cannot be explained otherwise.

The impact of land reform on the agrarian class structure has been uneven.It led to the eviction of smaller tenants as is evident from the decline in the percentage of holdings reporting land lease.For the years 1953-54, 1960-61 and 1961-62 the corresponding all India figures of land lease are 39.85, 27.33 and 23.52 percent. There is decline in successive years. This trend is confirmed for Hyderabad by A.M.Khusro's study which revealed that land reform led to marked decline in tenancy and growth of owner cultivators. In this process the eviction of the share croppers and oral tenants caused hardship to and rural poor. Smaller tenants received much less protection and suffered more by evictions than the bigger ones. Dandekar in his study of the Bombay state came across cases of extensive resumption and continued dominance of land lords over their tenants. In Gujarat, the study of M.B.Desai and R.S.Mehta reveals that if land reform gave owner ship of land to some tenants these also created the new phenomenon of 'concealed tenacy' and occupancies which perpetuates the agrarian class differences. Similarly in West Bengal the baragader's fate remains uncertain for getting an opportunity of cultivate land. It depends upon the landlord's assessment of the 'Political situation'. Even when the baragaders are allowed to cultivate land the same is continually shifted as not to allow any permanent interest of the baragaders to develop over the land. The situation is the same in he states of Bihar and Andhra Pradesh (see A.M.Khusro, 1958:V.M.Dandekar and G.S.Khudanpur,1957; Desai and Mehta 1969; National sample surveys Nos. 30,122,146 etc.).

The uneven nature of the impact that the land reformer have had on the agrarian classes leads one to question who has benefited from the land reforms and developmental changes in the agrarian system in India ? Has the landlord benefited most or has a new class of peasants emerged in the country side which has reaped the maximum benefits? There is a view that the landlords have come off the best (see.D. Warriner, 1969), but the comparative data show that the real benificiaries are the intermediate class of peasant, who have replace the older Zamindars in matters of economic as well as political power in the country side. In Utter Pradesh for example, the traditional zamindars who were mostly Rajputs, Brahmans, or Bhumihars are now being increasingly overwhelmed in economic as well as political competition by the middle class peasants belonging to the Ahir, Kurmi and other intermediate castes. The power of the feudal families is, of course, on the decline all over the country.

The trends in the agrarian class structure and relationships have been summarised by P.C.joshi as (1)" the decline of feudalistic and Customary types of tenancy and its replacement by more exploitative and insecure lease arrangements;(2) the increasing importance of commercial tenancy based on the rich and middle strata of the peasantry who are part owners and part tenants and possess resources and enterprise for dynamic agriculture, and (3) the decline of feudal landlords and the rise of commercially oriented landlords either functioning as owner farmers or utilising the mode of a new, non-customary type of tenancy for dynamic the pursuit of agriculture as business proposition" (P.C.Joshi, 1971). The emergence of the commercial peasants has led to two important socio-economic consequences in the country, first, it has increased the efficency and productivity of agriculture and has led the country to what is popularly called 'green revolution' but, secondly, the process of agricultural capitalism in villages assoicated with the decay in the fortunes of the poor peasantry and the agricultural labourers has also accentuated class conflicts and tensions in various parts of the country. In fact, the prosperity of few magnifies the poverty of the many and leads to social discontentment. This is further enlarged into class movements and radical political mobilisation. Thus, cumulative or 'value added' process of agrarian unrest tends to operate which has far reaching social and political implications.

Ever since the British started interfering with the land tenures in India by restructuring the traditional land systems, opposition had been expressed by the adversed peasants in violent or non-violent form. To meet such situations one of the practices of the colonial governement had been to introduce reforms through enactment within the framework of the general land policy which they had adoped. As such land reforms through legislation originated in the British period and the same was continued by the Indian leadership.

After the introduction of the permanent settlement, such regulations were enacted which enabled the zamindars to exploit their raiyat with all the nicety of an oppression. First such regulation enacted by the Government was the notorious haftam or Regulation 7 of 1799 which gave the landlords practically unrestricted right of distraint. They were empowered, to distrain, without sending any notice to any court of justice or any public officer, the crops and products of the earth of every description, the gram, castle and all other personal property, whether found in the house or on the premises of any other persons. This regulation further strengthened the hands of zmindars in exploiting the raiyats and it was very injurious to the peasants and cultivatiors. There is scarcely a country in the civilised word, remarked, filed, in which a landlord is allowed to evict his tenant without having recourse to the regular tribunals, but the Bengal zamindar was deliberately told by the legislature that he was at liberty to out his tenants if the rents claimed by him were in arrear at the end of the year, leaving them to recover their rights, if infringed, by having recourse to those new and untried courts of justice, the failure in which might be punished with fine or imprisonment.

Thus, there can hardly by any doubt that the Haftam was very injurious to the cultivatiors and tenants. This regulation virtually handed over the tenantry to the landlords and they could raise rents at their pleasure. The property of the raiyats could by sold at the pleasure of the zamindar under the Haftman Regulations.

The regulations that followed this condemned system of notorious Haftam were no less rapacious and oppressive. The Panjam Regulations of 1912 (Regulation V. of 1812) and Regulation XI of 1822 strengthened the oppressive hands of zamindars. As has been well observed, under the Haftam process the person of the ryot could be seized in default; the Panjam process his property could be distrained; and in either case the proceedings commenced with what has been described as a strong presumption equivalent to a knock down below against. The ryot. These land laws proved to be very disadvantageous to the cultivatiors. They were designed primarily to serve the interests of the zamindars and the Government. Strengthened by these land laws the landlords let loose a reign of oppression on the raiyats and they were assisted in this nefarious game of exploitation and extortions by the British imperialists, whose primary concern was to receive punctual revenue from the zamindars to consolidate their imperialist desings in India.

Thus, up to the middle of the 19th century, the zamindars exercised an authority over the raiyats far greater than that given to them by the original settlement of 1773. A revulsion of feelings developed against the working of these Regulations and the agraian discontent appeared among the oppressed and suppressed, which compelled the Government to enact 'Rent Act of 1859' which can be described as the first tenant law, directed towards the, amelioration of the oppressed raiyats' pitable conditions. The act defined the classes of tenants whose rent was fixed and conferred a right of ocupancy of those who had continuously held the same land for twelve years either personally or through their predecessors from whom the holding descended. But this Act also failed in mitigating the sufferings of the poor peasants in absence of village records and consequently, the raiyats had great difficulty in proving possession over their land for twelve years continusously. Added to this difficulty was the practice of the zamindars to change the land in possession of raiyats before twelve years had expired in order to prevent accrual of raiyats occupancy rights.

During the next two decades, the Rent Act also proved to be unworkable and ineffective in practice and the Government, under rising tempo of agrarian discontent, enacted tenancy Act of 1885 to mitigate the sufferings of tenants and cultivators. The two main objects of this Act were to extend the right of occupancy to settled cultivators. But this Act accepted the rights of zamindars to enhance rents in case of the increased value of the produce of the soil. No doubt, certain safeguards were provided against the enhancement of rent but they proved to be ineffective in practice and the Act failed to check the rapacious zamindars in enhancing rent without proper grounds which resulted in the exploitation of the raiyats.

The extent of exploitation becomes plain to see when we consider the exhorbitant amount of rents collected by the zamindars. The total revenue of Government fixed under the permanent settlement for Bengal, Bihar and Orissa of 1793 was Rs. 2,85,87,772. The gross rental of raiyats was at that time not more than four crores, but the zamindars collected Rs. 16.5 crores from the cultivators as rent. According to the original engagement of 1793 the Government was supposed to receive 90% of the total collections and the zamindars keeping only 10% of it. As such the zamindars were entitled to 40 lakhs of rupees, whereas they took about 12.5 crores of rupees. This shows that the raiyats were forced to pay thirty time more to the zamindars than their due for the collection of revenue.

In addition to this, cultivators were exploited by zamindars in various other ways by imposing different types of abwabs, nazarans, salami etc. When the permanent settlement was concluded, many of the old abwabs were consolidated with the rent and fresh abwabs were prohibited. But imposition and collection of illegal abwabs continued unchecked. Illegal abwabs were imposed by rapacious zamindars for marrying their daughter, bying an elephant, going on religious trips and for variety of functions.Rajendra Prasad in his book "Satyagrah in Champaran" has enumerated as many as forty kinds of abwabs which were realised by the zamindars and indigo planters in Champaran. Despite the fact that levying of abwabs was prohibited by the tenancy Act, Zamindars all over the permanently settled areas levied and collected them with utmost rapacity.

That exploited and oppressed peasants of India in general and of Bihar in particular had for long been bearing various evils of an unjust land system. The peasant movement as such was the product of accumulated grievances of the down-trodden and exploited peasantry under a system of land tenure which was oppressive, exploitative and rapacious. Alien domination was certainly an evil, and the zamindari system which it created, nourished and patronised, was the parent of acute hardships for the peasants, who like dumb driven cattle toiled and tilled the fruit of which went into the coffers of their landlord masters, most of them were absentees, spending their days and nights amidst the varied attractions of the cities.

Peasant unrest and uprisings in their primitive forms found expression in isolated actions of revenge and violence against individual money lenders and landlords. Outstanding episodes of ; pleasants uprisings in the latter part of the nineteenth century were:the santhal Insurrection (14855-56): the Indigo cultivators strike (1860): the Bengal peasant Uprisings in Pabna and Bogra (1872); the Maratha peasant Uprisings (1875-76) and the Mopan Uprisings (1836-96). (Indian Nation March 13,1956). They were manifestations of the genuine grivances of the peasants and workers against and oppression and high handednes of land lords, moneylenders and indigo-planters.

But all these uprisings and agitations by the peasants were only isolated, spasmodic and unsystematic endeavours which resulted, in some areas, in the mitigating of the immediate grievances of the peasantry. Systematic espousing of the peasants'cause, organised agitations and representation of the peasants needs and demands and authentic and painstaking investigation of the root causes of peasants difficulties came for the first time under the inspiring leadership of Mahatma Gandhi in the Champaran Satyagrah Campaign. Bardoli no-tax campaing was the second achievement of the peasants under the leadership of Mahatma Gandhi and Sardar Vallabh Bhai Patel.

Non-cooperation and civil Disobedience movements awakened the rural masses and made them resolute to fight against the oppression inflicated upon by an unjust and rapacious land system. These movements of national awakening coincided with a very grave economic crisis in agrarian society, added and abtted by the great Depression that had occurred in the early years of 1930's. Sharp slump in the prices of agricultural products accentuated the hardships of the peasants, already groaning under an inhuman land-relationship. Such a situation, unique and unprecedented in its severity, possessed all the essential requisities to produce and organised peasant movement. Coming events cast their shadow before, and Jawaharlal Nehru hinted about the coming possibility."The wind is blowing to the village and to the mudhuts were well our poverty-striken, peasantry and it is likely to become a hurricans if relief does not come to them soon. All our political problems and discussions are but the background for the outstanding and overwhelming problem of India the land problem."

"Land to the tiller" has been a widely accepted principle of agrarian reforms in our country in the post independence era.This principle implies conferment of occupancy rights to those who are actual tillers of the soil. To put it differently, this intends to make actual cultivators of the owners of the land they cultivate. This objective has been sought to be achieved by tenancy laws hither to enacted by the Governement in favour of the actual tillers of the soil.

Whatever might have been the intentions of the farmers of the permanent settlement Regulations, the land now belonged to the new class of land lords as proprietors and cultivators were virtually converted into tenants at will under the permanent settlement, the cultivators position was underfined and the onus; of proving whether the produce rent demanded but the zamindari was proper or not was thrown on the tenants. The tenants, in absence of documentary evidence regarding rate of rents,succumbed to demands of landlords and fell into arrears of rent. In absence of underfined pargana rates of rents zamindars more often resorted to rackrenting their tenants. Owing to difficulty in recovery of rents, the zamindars farmed out the villages to other persons. Thus, many layers of intermediary interests grew between the Governement and actual tillers of the soil. Even subsequent Regulations of 1799 and 1812 did not mitigate the oppressions of the tenants but on the other hand, they aided and abetted the oppressions ;penetrated on the tenants and placed the tenants practically at the mercy of landlords. Their property was liable to distraint and their person to imprisonment, if they failed to pay their rent to the landlords, however, exorbitant it might be. The tenants continued to be rack-rented, impoverished and oppressed until the passing of the Rent Act of 1859. This Act restrained the landlords power of rent enhancement in certain cases. In place of the old classification of raiyats having no such rights, i.e., tenants at will. (Regulations on 1799 and 1812 and the Rent Act of 1859).

In order to adumbrate the genesis of rural tension of Bihar it will be pertient to furnish in detail, the agrarian trouble in different phases as it has not only proved a determinant factor but has one way or the other played a catalytic role in a generating and aggravating tension in rural areas of Bihar.

As for tenancy Act of Bihar is concerned there are three Tenancy Acts, namely the Bihar Tenancy Act, 1885. The Chhotanagpur Tenancy Act, 1908 and Santhal Pargana Tenancy (Supplementory Provisions) Act, 1949. Today, in most parts of the state the tenancies are mainly regulated by the Tenancy Act of 1885 with subsequent amendments and the land reforms (Fixation of ceiling Area and Acquisition of Surplus Land) Act, 1961. After the abolition of zamindari in the state tenants may be divided in to the following class:

(1) Non-occupancy raiyats (i.e.raiyats not having the right of occupancy).
(ii) Occupancy raiyats (i.e. raiyats having a right of occupancy in the land held by them).
(iii) Under-raiyats (i.e.tenants holding, immediately or mediately, under raiyats).

In the Chhotanagpur Division,there are two more classes of raiyats namely (1) Raiyats having Khunt Katti Rights and (ii) Mundari Khunti

Kattidars.

They are also called settled raiyats. A person who holds any land situated in a village for twelve years either himself or through inheritance, becomes settled raiyats of the village. Such a raiyat gets rights of occupancy in all lands for the time being held by him as raiyat in that village. (The Bihar tenancy Act 1885, clauses 20 and 21). An occupancy raiyat is entitled, under the provisions of the Tenancy Act of 1885, to use lands in any manner which does not materially impair the value of the land or render it unfit for the purpose of tenancy. (Bihar Tenancy Act 1934 cluse 23). An accupancy raiyat is repaired to pay rent to the landlord for his holding at fair and equitable rates. (Bihar Tenancy Act, 1934, clause 24). The rent is to be paid in cash or kind or partly in cash and partly in kind. When the rent is payable in kind, in part or whole, it might be commuted to entirely money rent on application of the raiyat or the landlord.

There are also provisions in the Tenancy Act of 1885, which protect occupancy raiyats from eviction from their land. An occupancy raiyat cannot be ejected by his landlords from his holding except in execution of a decree for ejectment passed on the ground; (The Bihar Tenancy Act 1885 clause 25).

(i) That he has used the land comprised in his holding in a manner which renders it unfit for the purpose of the tenancy; or
(ii) That he has broken a condition on breach of which he is, under the terms of contract between himself and his landlords, liable to be ejected.

Moreover, the rights of occupancy raiyats under the provisions of the Tenancy Act of 1885, are permanent, heritable and transferable. (The Bihar Tenancy Act, 1935 clause 26A). But the position relating to transferability of land in Santhal Parganas and in Chhotanagpur is different.

When a non-occupancy raiyat is admited to the occupation of land, he becomes liable to pay such rent as may be agreed on between himself and his landlord at the time of the admission. Under the provision of the Tenancy Act of 1885, the rent of a non-occupancy raiyat cannot be enhanced except by registered agreement or through court.

The Act provides some safeguards to a non-occupancy raiyat against his eviction by his landlord. The Act provides that a non-occupancy raiyat is liable to be ejected on one or more of the following grounds and not otherwise.

(i) On the ground that they failed to pay arrears of rent;
(ii) On the ground that he has used the land in a manner which renders it unfit for the purposes of tenancy, or that he has broken a condition on which he is under the terms of a contract between himself and his landlord to be ejected;
(iii) Where he has been admitted to occupation of the land under a registered lesse. On the ground that the term of the lease has expired.

The rights of non-occupancy raiyats are heritable but not transferable. A very small area of land is, however held by non-occupancy raiyats.

In the Bihar Tenancy Act of 1865, under raiyats (sharecroppers) have been recognised and the rates of rent recoverable from them by the landlord have been limited of an under raiyat holding at money rent in not entitled to recover rent exceeding the rent, which he himself pays, by more than the following percentage of the same namely;

(i) When the rent payable by the under-raiyat is payable under a registered lease or agreement fifty percent and
(ii) In any other case twenty five percent. (The Bihar Tenancy, Act, 1885, Clause 48C).

But prior to the amendment in the Tenancy Act of 1885 in the year 1955, there existed no provision in the Act fixing the limit to produce rent to be paid by an under-raiyat to his immediate landlord, which proved a source of considerable hardship to the former. The amending Act of 1955 held that when under-raiyats exceding seventieth of the produce.

In the Bihar Tenancy Act of 1885, there are also provisions relating to acquisition of right of occupancy by under-raiyat in any village for a period of twelve years, is deemed to have acquired a right of occupancy in any land, becomes entitled to the use of such land as on an occupancy raiyat. (The Bihar Tenancy Act, 1885, clause 98D).

The Tenancy Act also mentions the grounds on which an under raiyat without occupancy right can be ejected from his land.By his landlord on one or more of the following grounds and not otherwise (The Bihar

Tenancy Act, 1885, clause 49).

(i) On the ground that he has failed to pay an arrear of rent;
(ii) On the ground that he has used the land in manner which renders it unfit for the purpose of the tenancy, or that he has broken a condition on breach of which he is, under terms of a contract between himself and his landlord, liable to be ejected.

An under-raiyat with or with our occupancy rights in the lands held by him cannot be ejected from the land except in execution of a decree passed by a civil court. (The Bihar Tenancy Act, 1885, Clause 89).

Despite this legal position, lakhs of share-croprers in Bihar were ejected from their lands in the wake of zamindari abolition measures and even after.

The Bihar Tenancy Act of 1885 still continues in force in the state. Right from the enforcement since Ist November, 1885, a thirty two amendments have been made in the Act.(The Bihar Tenancy Act, 1885).Originally the Act contained 196 sections and three schedules, but since, 1885, all the schedules have been amended. The uniform object of these amendments, specially after the congress assumed the reigns of office in 1937 has been to bend the provisions of the Act in favour of tenants and share-croppers. After the installation of the first popular ministry in 1937, the Bihar Tenancy (Amendment)Acts of 1937 and 1938 were passed, which mitigated the oppressions and sufferings of the tenants to a considerable extent.

Since independence, twelve amendments have been made in the Tenancy Act of 1885 in different years and the latest amending act was passed in 1970 of these amendments, one passed in 1955, popularly known as Bataidari Act and the other in 1970 require special mention, for they aroused political controversies in the state on an unprecedented scale.

Of all the amending legislations to the Bihar Tenancy Act, 1885, this Amending Act was by far the most important as well as most controversial: because, the Act, intended to protect bataidars (sharecroppers) from their illegal ejectment and controversial because it evoked. Sharpest opposition from land interests in general and some members of the congress legislature party in particular. K.B.Sahay, the then Revenue Minister, while justifying the measures maintained; (the

Bihar Tenancy Amendment Bill, 1954, Bihar Gazette, Extraordinary, December 13, 1954).

Under the existing provisions of the Bihar Tenancy Act, 1885, an under-raiyat can be evicted from the land, held by him, on certain specified grounds only and his eviction can be effected in execution of a decree and not otherwise. As the provisions stand at present, an under raiyat, dispossed from his land without due compliance with requirements of law in this regard, is however left with no option but to seek recurse to civil court for being replaced in possession there of and he is thus put to serious disadvantages. With a view to obviating us difficulties in this regard, it is considered desirable to amend the provisions of the Act so that a collector is empowered to restore possession, in suitable cases, on his own motion or on application by the illegally evicted under raiyat, after a summary enquiry.

Bataidary system (share-cropping system), one of the features of Bihar's agrarian system is responsible to a great extent for the backwardness of the state's agriculture. This system cuts at the very root of better farming and deprives the actual tillers of the basic motivation for switching over from subsistence farming to commercial farming. (K.N.Prasad 1967, 416).

Although no separated figures are available for sharecroppers in the Census Reports of 1961 and 1971, but its wide scale prevalence can be better imagined, if one recalls that out of the total agricultural population of 34.6 millions in 1951, 8.8 millions were landless agricultural workers; 3.3. millions were under-raiyats and the rest occupancy raiyats. (K.N.Prasad:1967:416).

Under the existing provisions of the Bihar tenancy Act, Chotanagpur Tenancy Act and Santhal Pargana Regulations, the occupancy raiyats have been permanent and heritable rights in agriculture. Their status is hardly distingushable from those of the erstwhile landlords, particularly after the abolition of zamindars, as the Governement has itself replaced the landlords.

However, the abolition of zamindari in the state did not improve the conditions of share-croppers and under-raiyats). Until the Bihar Tenancy (Second Amendments) Act, 1955, an under-raiyat ejected by his landlord illegally from the land held by him did not have any option other than to go to the civil court. But as most of the share-croppers were economically depressed, they could not be in a position to meet the heavy expenses of a litigation in a civil court. The poor share-croppers were further handicapped due to the fact that landlords did not either execute any written lease in their favour of under-raiyats with the result that the former did not have any documentary proof to support their case in a law court. In order to protect share croppers from illegal ejectment the Bihar Tenancy Act was amended through the Bihar Tenancy (Second Amendment) Act, 1955. The Amending Act of 1955 provided for;

(i) Reduction in the share of produce, payable by a raiyat in kind. rent to his landlord from nine twentieth to five-twentieth of the produce; (Bihar Tenancy Act, 1885,Clause 178 B).

(ii) Fixation of seven-twentieth as the maximum share in produce realisable from an under raiyat on rent in kind by his landlord, (The Bihar Tenancy Act Clause 48 A) and

(iii) Empowering the collectors to take action for restoration of unlawfully ejected under-raiyats to their lands since February, 1, 1953 (The Bihar Tenancy, Act, 1885, 48 D).

Thus, under the provisions of the Amending Act, 1955, the maximum produce rent that could be realised from under-raiyat was fixed. The Act further provided that the landlord of an under raiyat would not be entitled to any share in the straw or Bhoosa as rent out of the produce of such land. The Act empowered the Collectors to take action either on their own inititave or on application for restoration of possession to under-raiyats, ejected unlawfully from their lands since February 1, 1953.

The select commitee, to which the Bihar Tenancy (Amendment) Bill, 1954 (which was later on enacted as Bihar Tenancy, Second Amendment Act, 1955) was referred, recommended for a concilliation Board. The purpose behind the constitution of concillation Board was to provide a machinery for amicable settlement of disputes between under-raiyats (share croppers) and landlord; but in case of the failure of the Board to settle disputes amicably, the records of the Bord were to be sent to the collectors, who in the prescribed manner, would restore the land to the evicted under raiyats, if they (collectors) considered that the under-raiyats had been illegally evicted.

The above provisions of the Bihar Tenancy (Amendment) Act, 1955 were intended to benefit under-raiyats. K.B.Sahay, the then Revenue minister, was quite justificed in calling the provisions of the Act as 'progressive and revolutionary '. (The searchlight October 14, 1955).

But this measure which touched the land inter was not without protest from among the members of the congress Legislature party and vested interests likely to be affected.

Tenancy (Amendment) Bill, 1954 was introduced by K.B.Sahay in the Legislative Assembly on December 13, 1954 in a special session of the legislature. Sahay wanted the Bill to be passed in the same session, but there was a fierce opposition to the proposed legislation from a section of the congress legislature party. One of the members of the congress legislature party. Ram Jeewan Mahto moved a contrary motion (as against the motion of Sahay to consider the bill which read as follows:

"That the Bihar Tenancy (Amendment) Bill, 1954 be referred to a select Commitee with instructions to report by the 31st Jaunary, 1955". (Bihar Legislative Assembly Debates 1954 Vol.6, No.1, December 13, 1954,153).

The motion for consideration and passage of the bill was supported by the members of the United Jharkhand Socialist Party and Independent Legislature Group. But quite surprisingly, K.B. Sahay himself veered round the motion of Mahto for its reference to a select Committee. This change in stand on the part of Sahay was bitterly criticised by the opposition members who expressed the view that under the pressure of the vested interests inside and outside the congress party he had to retrace his step.

The opposition charge was not without foundation. At the party meeting held on December 12, 1954 a powerful section of the congress legislature party was reported to have opposed the passage of the Bataidari Bill in the current session. (The Bihar Legislative Assembly Debates, 1954,181). Moreover, opposition to the measure come from some of the public men of the state, who did not want that occupancy right should accrue to under raiyat on such lands which were within the ceiling area. (The Searchlight December 12, 1954).

K.B.Sahay (the than Revenue Minister) had also to face reactionary press, conservative Bar-Associations and so called peasants organisations, Indian Nation, owned by one of the biggest landlords of the country was naturally critical of the proposed legislation. Several Bar-Associations of the state passed resolution against the passage of the measure. (The Searchlight, December 12, 1954). Further more, a meeting of the representatives of the land owing peasants was reported to have been held at the state capital to denounce the proposed bataidari legislation under the auspices of "Bihar Kisan Protection Committee. "The meeting through a resulution passed at the meeting characterised the proposed measure as crude method of catching votes at the time of the next general election drawing nearer. (The Searchlight 1955). The meeting was further of the opinion, "While incalculated and irreparable harm may be done to a section of kisans e.g. widows, orphans, old and disabled persons,shall tenants, petty Governement servants, small traders and low-income group professionals, it will not do good to the sub-tenants, the relations between whom and the Kisans upto this time have been most cordial. "(The Searchlight 1955). The meeting further resolved to sent a five-men delegation to represent the case of land owners and submit a memorandum to the president of India, the prime Minister and other in the Central cabinet as well as to the Bihar Governor, Chief Minister and the president of the All India Congress Committee. (The Searchlight 1955).

Despite these and other protests and opposition to the Bataidari legislation, the Bihar Tenancy (Second Amendment) Bill of 1954 was enacted into Act and this Amending Act came into force on December, 1955 after being assented to by the Governor of Bihar. (The Searchlight, Novemeber 24, 1955).

The Bihar Land Reforms Act, 1950 did not touch the tenant landlord relationship as the purpose of the Act was only to abolish the intermediaries. But the Ceiling Act, 1961 contains comprehensive provision concerning tenancy reforms. This was natural because after the abolition of zamindari in Bihar, there were now only two classes of tenants, namely raiyats and under raiyats. Raiyats were already enjoying comprehensive safeguards against evictions, exactions etc. The Tenancy (Second Amendment) Act of 1961 strengthened further the position of under raiyats.

The Ceiling Act permits subletting of lands by raiyat for a period, not exceeding seven years at a time after giving information to the collector or the Executive Commitee of the Gram Panchayat in the prescribed manner. (Bihar Land Reforms Fixation of ceiling area and acquisition of surplus land) Act, 1961, clause 20). Again only certain specified categories of raiyats (i.e. minor or disabled raiyats or unmarried or divorced women ect). are entitled to sublet their lands. (Bihar Land Reforms, Fixation of ceiling Area and Acquisition of Surplus Land Act, 1961, provision to claue 20). Having allowed subletting under certain conditions, the ceiling act reduces the amount of rent in kind payable by under-raiyats to raiyats subletting lands from seven twentieth to maximum of one fourth of the gross produce and the raiyat is not entitled to any share in the straw or bhoosa as rent out of the produce of the land sublet. (Bihar Land Reforms Fixation of Ceiling Area and Acquisition of surplus Land Act, 1961 sub clause 2 of clause 20). In case of Money rent, the Act, also places a limit on the maximum rent recoverable from an under raiyat i.e. maximum of fifty percent of the rent which a raiyat himself pays as land revenul. (Bihar Land Reforms Fixation of Ceiling Area in Acquisition of surplus land Act, 1961, sub -clause 2 of the clause 20).

The Ceiling Act of 1961 also makes provisions for acquisition of status of occupancy raiyats by under raiyats. Under raiyats on surplus land as well as within the Ceiling Area of raiyats are entitled to acquire status of raiyats under the provisions of the Act. (Bihar Land Reforms Fixation of Ceiling Area of and Aquisition of surplus Land Act 1961, clause 21 and 22). Every under raiyat of a raiyat, holding land in excess of the ceiling area, is deemed to have acquired the status of an occupancy raiyat provided the land is not lawfully resumed by the raiyat. (Bihar Land Reforms Fixation of Ceiling Area and Acquisition of Surplus Land Act, 1961 Clause 22).

Under the tenancy law in force in the state, the landlords of occupancy raiyats did not have any right of resumption for personal cultivation. So far as under raiyats were concerned, their landlords, were entitled to resume lands only on the expiry of the lease or on some other grounds, where lands were sublest by written lease. But under the Ceiling Act of 1961, raiyats possessing lands in excess of ceiling areas, are entitled to resume such lands for personal cultivation which may be in the possession of under raiyats, having no occupancy right.(Bihar Land Reforms Fixation of Ceiling Area and Acquisition of surplus Land Act, 1961, Clause 12). But this right of resumption on the raiyats is to be exercise in such a manner as not to leave less than five acres of land to the under-raiyat is less than ten acres, the area to be resumed by a raiyat from an under raiyat cannot exceed half of such total areas.(Bihar Land Reforms Fixation of Ceiling Area and Acquisition of surplus Land Act, 1961, provision to clause 12). But under raiyat is entitled to retain, on his option, at least one acre besides his homestead or the entire area of such land held by him if it is less than one acre. (Bihar Land Reforms Fixation of Ceilitng Area and Acquisition of surplus Land Act, 1961, Provision to clause 12).

Thus the Ceiling Act of 1961 contains certain provision which are advantageous to under tenants in as much as they can acquire the status of occupancy raiyats on surplus lands held by their land lords. But the right of resumption given to raiyats is equally injurious to the interests of under-raiyats and this right has been greatly abused by landlords, who have been using as an additional weapon in eviction the share-croppers.

No protection to share-croppers and under tenants can be afforded unless there is a proper record of rights. Evictions of under-raiyats on a large scale in the wake of zamindari abolition and even after were rampant. Despite the provisions of the Bihar Tenancy Act that no tenant or under tenant could be evicted from his land without a decree from the civil court, under raiyats were evicted on a big scale and the evicted under raiyats were handicapped in proving their claims in civil courts in absence of documentary evidences in view of the fact that large protions of lands held by under raiyats were on oral leases.

In order to protect under raiyats from evictions, the Governement of Bihar started a special drive in 1964 to record the names of under raiyats (share croppers) against the land in their cultivating possession in the field Bujharat records being prepared by the Revenure Department. When the drive was just beginning to take its stride, this recording was stopped by a confidential communication and officials violating these instruction were threatened with serious punishment. (New Age, October, 15 1967 and the Searchlight, 1964), the Governement issued a second Communication (No. SD/208/64-8603 dated 12th September, 1964) which directed as follows:

"Reports have been received about the evictions of under raiyats and other agrarian disturbances. Governement desire that every effort should be made to maintain peaceful relations between the raiyat and the under raiyat and requisite steps should be taken to avoid any action which may give rise to disorder. In order to achieve the same the collection of details to that extent should be kept in abeyance."(A.N.Seth, New Delhi, 1966, 48).

As a result, no steps were taken to record the names of subtenants and under raiyats in the field bujharat drive. This was in the words of Indradeep Sinha, former Revenue Minister of Bihar, not only a gross betrayal of the interests of the subtenants and share croppers but also a calculated violation of the provisions of the Bihar Tenancy Act which already conferred certain rights on subtenants.(Indradeep Sinha, 1967).

The above circular of the Governement imposed a ban on the recording of the names of under raiyats and share croppers.(But after the defeat of the Congress at polls in 1967 in the state and formation of the United Front Governement, once again the implementation of the existing tenancy laws affording certain protection to under raiyats and share-croppers was taken up.(The Searchlight, October, 18, 1967). With this end in view, the Revenue Department by a circular issued on 25 September, 1967 annulled the confidential circular No. 7349 dated the 12th August 1964 and circular No. 8603, dated 12th September, 1964. (K.Gopalan"Bihar U.P. Governement to protect tenants", New Age. October 15, 1967,7). Indradeep Sinha, the then Revenue Minister, got the implementation circulars issued on October 3, 1967 under the Bihar Tenancy Act, the Santhal parganas Tenancy Act and on December 15, 1967 under the Homestead Tenancy Act (Indradeep Sinha 1968). These circulars provided for the following: (Indradeep Sinha, 1968).

(i) No Bataidar could be evicted without a decree from a court of law;
(ii) No landlord would interfere the harvesting of the crop sown by the share croppers;
(iii) No landlord could demand more than seven twentieth of the produce and any portion of the straw as his share;
(iv) The illegal ban on the recording of the share croppers imposed by K.B.Sahay in October, 1964 stood cancelled.
(vi) Alienation of the non-transferable lands of the Santhals and other Adivasis would be cancelled and the lands so alienated would be restored to the original tenants;
(vii) A special drive would be launched to record the existing home-steads.

As soon as the move to implement the above items was initiated a storm of protest was raised through the press and political platform. The Jana Sangh, one of the constituents of the United Front, started opposing the more for implementing the Bataidari laws.Thakur Prasad, the then President of the Bihar Jana Sangh called upon "the citizens and farmers of Bihar to defend their life, properties, farms and families with lathies (bamboo-sticks) in hand instead of depending upon the police to defend them". (The Searchlight, October 23, 1967). The Jana Sangh members of the united front Government held several public meetings in the state to oppose the implementation of Bataidari laws. The move was supported by the Jan Kranti Dal of Kamakhya Narain Singh one of the constituents of the United front Government. Some congress leaders also extended their support in opposing the Bataidari laws. Mahesh Prasad Sinha, the then leader of the Bihar Congress Legislature party, warned the Governement not to take up the implementation of the Bataidari law as the implementation of the Bataidari law as the Bataidari Scheme was fraught with danger.(The Searchlight,December 7, 1967).

Satyendra Narayan Sinha warned the United Front Governement "not to take any hasty action to enforce the Batairari Law."(The Indian Nation, November 13, 1967).

Such oppositions to the Bataidar law created a sort of apprechension that the implementation of the Bataidari provisions of the Bihar Tenancy Act would result in accrual of accupancy rights to share croppers. To clear the apprehension, a clarification was issued on the radio and throughout the press.(Indradeep Sinha, O.P.Cit.,13). The clarification was in the nature of a proposal to amend section 48C of the Bihar Tenancy Act so as to allow small land owners, the right to resume their land for self cultivation. The Jana Sangh leaders supported by some other leaders of the United Front and the congress, declared to oppose the proposed amendment to the Tenancy Act, tooth and nail. A sharp controvery arose among the constituent parties of the United Front Governement with regard to the proposed amendment to section 48C.of the Bihar Tenancy Act. As a result the proposed Amending ordinance and later on the Bill got struck in the co-ordination Committee and the Cabinet.

Thus, during the first United Front Ministry, all attempts to implement the tenancy laws and make suitable amendments to the Bihar Tenancy Act, 1885 were watered down in face of fierce opposition from the Jana Sangh, the jan Kranti Dal and leaders belonging to Congress and the Sanyukta Socialist Parties. (Pranav Chatterjee, the Searchlight, November 24, 1967) All Political parties, except the Communist Party wanted to postpone the implementation of tenancy laws, relating to bataidari-rights of under-raiyats and sub-tenants on one ground or the other. As such, the Revenue Minister, Indradeep Sinha, could not marshal sufficient support to enforce the tenancy rights of share croppers and underrights.

The proposed amendment to the Bihar Tenancy Act, which was forestalled during the first United Front Governement could be enacted in 1970. The Amending Act of 1970 amended section 48c of the Bihar Tenancy Act, an under raiyat was entitled to acquire occupancy right on such lands, which he held continously as an under raiyat for a; period of twelve years. (The Bihar Tenancy Act, 1885 Section 48C). This provision of the Act did not exclude any land owner land occupancy rights could accrue to under-raiyats on all lands whether such lands belonged to big land owners or small ones.

The Amending Act 1970 extended protection to small land owners and held that no occupancy right would acorue to an under-raiyat(irrespective of the period for which the land owners specifically), landowners could hold (on which occupancy owners) specifically; land owners could hold (on which occupancy right would not accrue to an under raiyat) at least five acres of land irrigated by flow, irrigation, lift irrigation, or tubewells, whether such irrigational facilities were owned constructed, maintained or improved by the Central Government or the State Government were owned and maintained by the landlord: or (b) ten acres of other land. (Provision to clause 48C of the Bihar Tenancy Act, 1885, substituted by section 2 of the Bihar Tenancy (Amendment Act, 1970, Bihar Act 8 of the 1970 for the original provision).

The Amending Act provided additional protection to land owners who could be classified as widows, persons suffering from mental or physical disability or persons in the army, navy and air force of the Indian Union (Sub clause (ii) of clause 48C of the Bihar Tenancy Act 1885).

The above provisions, as they seem apparently, have not been designed to benefit landlords and raiyats at the cost of under raiyats and share croppers.Instead, it is argued, such provisions will lessen fears prevalent even among small land owners that their occupancy right in certain lands may be threatened by their tenants and share croppers. Moreover, it is considered to be a pragmatic step as this will strike a unity among small land owners, under raiyats and landless labourers against landlords and big landholders. This will also reduce tension in rural areas between landlords and tenants.

Tenancy rights of under raiyats (share-croppers) were protected further by another section of the Amending Act, of 1970. Section 98E of the Bihar Tenancy Act, inserted by way of amendment in 1955 with the avowed objective of preventing evictions of under tenants and share-croppers,remained ineffective because it did not provide for restoration of the land after the sub tenant has actually been evicted. This was serious loophole in the existing Tenancy legislation.

In order to plug this loophole, section 48E of the Tenancy Act has been amended by section 3 of the Tenancy (Amendment) Act of 1970.

Which provides that an under raiyat, threatened with unlawful ejectment from his tenancy of by his landlord. (Substituted by section 3 of the Bihar Tenancy (Amendment) Act 1970 (Bihar Act 8 of 1970) for the original section 48E) can be protected by the intervention of a collector either on his own or in response to an application submitted to him by an under-raiyat pervious provisions in the Bihar Tenancy Act, 1885 would have permitted the intervention of the collector to settle dispute between a landlord and his tenant only after the eviction had taken phase.

Thus, the Tenancy (Amendment)Act of 1970 has been enacted with a view to safe guarding the interests of under-raiyats and under-tenants. The Amending Act has empowered the collector to take cognizance even of the threatened eviction of share croppers. Moreover, the Act has provided a great relief to small land owners, who were under a constant fear of losing the occupancy rights over lands, leased even temporarily under some pressing circumstances.

Attempt of the Government in the post independence era have been to bend the provisions of the Tenancy laws in favour of tenants and under tenants. Under various amendments to the Bihar Tenancy Act, 1885 (before the abolition of the Zamindari system the position of occupancy raiyats were safeguarded. Occupancy-raiyats were enjoying permanents, heritable and alienable rights over their lands. So only status quo has been maintained in their case. Attention of the Government was drawn towards strengthening the vulnerable position of under raiyats and share croppers, when in the wake of zamindari abolition and land ceiling Act, several lakhs of Bataidars (share-croppers) were evicted illegally from lands in their possession, for affording additional protections to under raiyats and share croppers, the Bihar Tenancy Act of 1885 was amended mainly in 1955 and 1970.

But the question arises: have the attempts of the Government resulted in real benefit to under raiyats and share croppers ? studies under taken on this issue have reveled that very little or practically no benefits have accrued to bataidars (share croppers) and under tenants. The working group land Reforms of the National Commission on Agriculture made a filed visit to two blocks of Madhubani and Muzaffarpur district in April 1973. The working group enquired and found that not a single Bataidar was recorded during the survey and settlement field operation, which was concluded in those areas only recently. (The Bihar Tenancy (Second Amendment)Act, 1955 (Bihar Act 24 of 1955). The working group maintained, "no law, however good it may be in conferring on paper right, own capable of not only defending their own rights given by the law, but also capable of mounting counter-action to prevent and forestall any direct attack on them... without this, the gap between promise and performance would become gradually wider and ultimately, unbridgeable, leaving no alternative for the required social change, excepting perhaps, through a major social convulsion."(Planning Commission Report of the Task Force on Agrarian Relations, New Delhi, 1973, 25).

Thus, the fact that no Bataidar (share-cropper) was recorded inspite of thd law lends weight to the criticism that in Bihar the Congress Government or other non-congress government lacked the required will to implement tenancy laws and the party in power was not sincerely committed to tenancy reforms, concerning security of tenure to under raiyats and share croppers.

Even the other benefits that have been provided to under raiyats and share croppers under tenancy laws are not still in practice in the state. The Bihar Tenancy Act, 1885 maintains that the produce rent payable to the landlord by an under raiyat will not exceed seven twentieth of the gross produce and the landlords will have no share in straw or bhoosa but the common practice of fifty-fifty share in produce is still in vague.

Moreover, legislations, offering certain protective and ameliorative privileges have been enacted but no necessary conditons for their implementation have been created. The first essential conditions for their implementation is that those who are to be benefited must be aware of laws offering such benefits. There should be organised efforts on the part of the Government to make share-croppers and under raiyats familiar with the provisions of the Acts. But there is a complete absence of organised efforts on the part of the Government to educate the beneficiarics, who are mostly ignorant of the provisions of the Tenancy Acts.

Socio-economic weaknesses of share-croppers and under tenants are one of the major reasons for the non-implementation of tenancy laws.

Most of the share croppers and under tenants are socially backward and economically depressed. As a result they fail to protect their rights in face of aggressive postures from their landlords. Legal rights conferred on share croppers have failed to guarantee security to tenany. The Task Force of the planning Commission discussion the futility of legal security of tenancy has asserted,"There is nothing to prevent a determined group of landlords from adopting other method to throw out physically from the land, the share croppers who have the temerity to get themselves recorded as tenants."

In addition to the above reasons, the attitude of the bureaucracy towards the implementation of the agrarian reforms in general and tenancy reforms in particular is often lukewarm and apathetic. Land holder, in eviction share croppers and under raiyats from their lands are generally aided and abetted by Government officials, as most of them are themslves substantial landholders or they have close links with big land owners.

Finally, the resumption clauses of the ceiling Act of 1961 have led to widespread ejections of share croppers and under raiyats. By allowing the land holder to resume lands from his tenants for personal cultivation the Act permits the eviction of under raiyat or tenants from lands they have been tilling without being accorded occupancy raiyat status.

The system of share-cropping which is prevalent in part of Bihar has several sinister aspect. The land owners do not allow the share-croppers to cultivate the same land in successive years. This is be cause of the fear among the land owners that if the share croppers are allowed to cultivate the same land in consecutive years, they may state take their claim for occupancy rights. Though according to land, the land owner is entitled to only 1/4 of the produce, in fact the land owners insist and take half the produce with no security of tenre and no bargaining power, the share croppers are entirely at the mercy of the land owners. Most of the share-croppers belong to down trodden community. In some of the districts of Bihar, the share-cropping system has given rise to considerable rural tensions culminating in bloodshed.

Anand Chakravarti writing in the Economic and Political weekly dated 25, March 1986 has observed that the belligerence of the land owners in general in contemporary Bihar is so very blatant that even the working committee group on land reforms of the National Commission on Agriculture had observed on the basis of experience in some areas of Bihar that land owners are organised and aggressive..with an obliging administration on their side, they are definetely not going to give up an iota of their rights, privileges and economic dominance without a stiff fight.. no law, nowever, good if may be in conferring on paper, right, title and interest on the bataidars, will have the slightest chance of success unless the bataidars have strong and militant mass organisation of their own, capable of not only defending their own rights given by the law—but also capable of mounting counter action to prevent and forestall any direct attack on them.

According to the report brought out by the revenue and land reforms department of the government of Bihar, for the position with regard to the disposal of cases envolving the share-croppers is, total cases which related to the share croppers were 58860 of which 16622 cases were decided in favour of Bataidars (Share-croppers) 33283 were decided against Bataidars and the cases pending were 8955.

Thus, we may conclude that some important changes in the Tenancy laws have been incorporated in favour of share croppers and under raiyats in the post Independence period in the state. But whenever the Government initiates any amendment to the Tenancy laws which affects the status quo in tenancy relationship, it cccasions protests and opposition from the vested interests. Whatever has been done till now is in the nature of compromise, effected between two diametricaly opposed group one standing for sweeping changes in tenancy reforms and the other opposed to any change in them. Secondly any attempt for reforms is bagged down under the weight of agitations and disturbances in the country side. The very declaration of the intention that some changes are contemplated in the field of tenancy relations to afford security and additional rights to under raiyats and share-croppers leads to agitations and distrubances in the country side. Thirdly, even most of the parties who swear day in and day out, in the name of radical agrarian reforms and welfare of share-croppers and landless, do not hesitate to shelve the issue, when called for to demonstrate their commitment. Lastly the parties of the Right wage fieree opposition to any change in the sphere of tenancy reforms. Their opposition to tenancy laws is aided and abetted by vested interests entrenched in any political pary inside and out side. Despite these built in depressors, some important changes made in the tenancy laws of the state, conferring security of tenure to share croppers and under tenants in the post independence era, to be appreciated. Rents that under-raiyats have to pay to their land owners now are fixed at a sufficiently low level. Under raiyats can acquire right of ownership on surplus lands of land owners, occupancy rights can accrue to under raiyats and share croppers on some lands under certain conditions. These provisions, if sincerely implemented are likely to imporve the conditions of tenants and share croppers in a considerable measure.

It is this action which is taking place in many parts of Bihar today.

The action is sporadic and spontaneous. And it is faced with brutal repression by the landlords, rich peasants and the state. In many instances it takes the form of caste, rather than class conflict. In some cases the former allies and even leaders of the poor peasantry have become its oppressors and it is not uncommon that yesterdays substantial tenants are today killing poor peasants, burning their miserable huts and raping their women. On the face of it, the situation of the poor peasants, agricultural labourers and other toiling people in Bihar is changing. 'And yet it moves'.

The prime concern of social scientists has been with the patterns of inequality and conflict as they occur due to the changing land relations whereas administrators have studied the "law and order" problems involved in such conflicts. Some generalizations have been offered by these inquiries to which we shall turn now.

In the first place, it has been suggested that the discrepancy between the egalitarian social norms and conservative distribution norms upheld by the poorer and dominant sections of society respectively is the primary casuse of agrarian unrest. The second point of view attempts to relate agrarian tension to the socio economic consequences of land reforms. And still another explanation is provided by those who sought its explanation in the adoption of new agricultural strategy since independence.

Beteille's concepts of "harmonic" and "disharmonic" social systems provide a good framework within which the problem of increasing agrarian unrest can be studied. (Andre Beteille, 1971). A harmonic social system is one in which there is consistency between the existential order and normative order; inequalities not only exist in fact but are also accepted as legitimate.(Andre Beteille, 1971). Thus it has been suggested that as society moves from a harmonic to a disharmonic system, it will face problems of tension and unrest. When we watch our contemporary agrarian scene it does mean that India particularly is passing through this stage.

A concise scheme to study organized protests has further been attempted by Beteille where he suggests three sets of factors which determine relations between groups and classes.(Andre Beteille, "The causes of Agrarian Unrest, "The Citizen, 1,23,1971,16-18)." These are (i) the conditions of existence, (ii) the consciousness of these conditons, and (iii) the political organization of this consciousness". When these factors develop in a particular direction, an organized peasant resistance emerges disturbing the existing power equations in the rural areas.

Essentially similar but comparatively elaborate analysis has been undertaken by common who has recognized the enormity and complexity of the problem. (T.K. Oommen, 1971,99-103). While characterizing the approach which attempts to correlate the growing agrarian tension to the increased disparity caused by green revolution as naive and simple he has held the following factors responsible for agrarian conflict:

(1) Perception of prevalent disparities in income by the rural poor,(2) A viable numerical strength of the agriucltural labour force and their consciousness of the political bargaining power, (3) the existence of an adequate support structure provided by political parties, (4) the rising aspirations of the rural masses, and (5) the increasing lack of fit between the socio-political framework and the economic order.(T.K.Oommen, 1971, 99-103). Developing his ideas further in another study, he has suggested that disparity is a necessary but not a sufficient conditon for tensions to crupt. (T.K.Oommen. 1971, 224-68).

The agrarian conflicts in several parts of the country have taken forms of ideological and class conflicts which reveal an important dimension of the problem, conflict between labourers and landowners is essentially a conflict between the radical and conservative ideologies. Alexander shows that in the Kainakari Pànchayat of Alleppey district of Kerala politicization of labourers has resulted in acute conflict between labourers and farmers. (K.C.Alexander, 1975). Hence he doubts if mere granting of higher wages to agricultural labourers could buy lasting peace in agrarian relations in Kuttanad. Although one can broadly agree with the general framework of Alexander's study, it is hard to accept his generalization about the existence of an egalitarian ideology as a sufficient conditions to arouse poeple's consciousness in the Indian countryside. A similar argument has been put forward in another study conducted in Tamil Nadu but here Alexander's claim of an experimental inquiry has proved to be a myth (K.C.Alexander, 1975). He starts with a claim to be entirely objective but finishes with a tone of social workers pleading with authority for sympathy to be shown to the agricultural labourers.

Ideological and class dimensions of the agrarian relations have also been emphasized in a study from Uttar Pradesh. While studying theland grab movement in Besti District launched in 1970. Singh has come to the conclusion the "even when necessary objective conditions to produce and sustain peasant revolts may not be present, a change in the subjective perception of injustice, exploitation and poverty may provide the basis of Peasant Mobilisation for a partial revolt."(Rajendra Singh 1974,44-70). All this strongly contests the suggestion that Indian peasantry suffers from; passivity, over-tolerance, immobility and such other trails.

The second major generalization with regard to the peasant unrest in post independent India strives to correlate it to the socio-economic consequences of land reforms. A radical transformation of the outmoded agrarian structure through numerous steps has been the basic objective of land reform measures undertaken by government since independence. It has also been a major plank of campaign of several political parties involved in peasant mobilization and militant peasant action. Besides land reforms "From Above" through legislations, another pattern has been an attempt to transfer "From below" through militant action as in the case of Telegana and Naxalbari movements. Variants of these experiments were seen in West Bengal CPI (M) led left front Government where legislative enactments are combined with peasant mobilization from below as in the case of the "controlled land seizure" still another attempt is seen in the Bhoodan and Gramdan movements under which persuasion of landlords and peaceful pressure by peasants are brought to induce changes in land relations. Unfortunately, no serious efforts have been made to study the impact of these experiments with the only exception of the evaluation of land reform legislations and their implementation. This gap has to be bridged if a proper and comprehensive evaluation of changing agrarian relations is required. (P.C. Joshi, 1977).

Several studies on the socio-economic impact of land reforms have been undertaken by Joshi in which he has not only analyzed the class character of land reforms but has attempted to show how these changes denote new and more obvious sources of social tension and conflict. (P.C.Joshi, 1970).Summarizing the overall impact of these measures in India and Pakistan he notes:-

> "... agrarian policy has been one of the factors accelerating the disintegration of the traditional agrarian system in these countries but without yet substituting any this stable and viable in the place. Agrarian reform itself has contributed both as ideology and as programme towards accentuating social tensions and distrubances in old security arrangements."(P.C.Joshi, 1974).

The Government of India has also recongnized the increasing agrarian tension in rural India due to the unfavourable socio-economic impact of land reforms. The Ministry of Home Affairs released its off-quoted report on the causes and nature of agrarian tension in August, 1969 and admitted that "programmes so far implemented are still more favourable to the large owner farmer than to the small tenant farmer". (Government of India. The causes and policy division, Ministry of Home Affairs, 1969). It boldly accented that as for the sharecropper and the landless labourer, they have been more often not, left out in the cold and in consequence of the these factors, disparities have wideened accentuating social tension.

Thus, by making provisions for different land reform measures, the Government accepted the principle of agrarian change in favour of the small peasants, share croppers and landless labourers. However, in the absence of their effective implementation a new wave of tension has erupted in rural areas. (M.N.Karna 1981).

Jannuzi has included a sizeable chapter on the growth of agrarian tension in Bihar in his work on the agrarian crisis. (F.T.Jannuzi, 1974). He examines the context of rural 'apathy'in the 1950's awakening of the Bihar peasants during the subsequent years. The study concentrates on the analysis of factors like governments failure to implement agrarian reforms and the changing social scene in rural areas on the one hand and agricultural production maximization focus and rapid population growth on the other. One may not fully subscribe to the stand taken by Jannuzi at several stages of his arguments. Neverthless, his explication of mounting tension in rural Bihar in the context of agrarian reforms cannot be ignored, "The immediate prospect in Bihar is for increasingly radical talk about the need for agrarian reforms, with little action in the filed of implementation."(F.T.Jannuzi, 1974,157).

A close look at these studies besides several others (Some important studies in the area are: Baljit Singh, Next step in village India, Asia Publishing House, Bombay 1961, Doreen Warriner, Land Reform in Principles and Practice, Oxford, India 1969, Sunil Sen. Agrarian changes in Punjab". Mainstream, fourteenth Annual Number, 1976; T.K.Oomen, "Agrarian Legislations and Movements as sources of chagge, the case of Kerala, "Economic and political weekly, X,40, October 4, 1975) more than suggests that the land reform measures have failed to remove the basic inequalities of our age-old agrarian structure. They further highlight the inherent character of our Governmental measures which outwardly profess help to the rural poor but essentially go against them. So long as such a situation continues or rural areas will not be free from monting tension. This brings us to the discussion of our last generalisation which identified another factor causing frastration, his tension, conflict and discontent among the rural poor.

It is no longer a disputable point that various land reforms legislations enacted since independence have proved merely to be a paper exercise. The main objective of distributing surplus land accuring from legislation on ceiling among the landless Harijans has not been realised.

A number of causes can be attributed to this failure. We have no intention to go into them. However one of the most important reasons has been defective legislation and its implementation. The land reform acts themsleves have been porous with the result that land owner has managed to pass through them without much efforts. Secondly, there has been lacking a political will to implement even emaciated land legislation firstly because the legislators by and large themselves belong to the landed gentry and secondly because there has always been the lurking fear that implementation might result in loss of votes.

Whatever be the reason there is little doubt that in the the state of Bihar all government of whatever hue and colour have been unable to tackle this very ticklish issue. It has, therefore, been allowed to drift. No better example of this drift can be cited than in the related enactment of land ceiling laws and still their tardy and dilatory implementation; and their virtual sabotage expressed through various loopholes. The Bihar land Reforms (Fixation of ceiling Area and Acquisition of Surplus land) Act of 1961 which was a diluted version of the 1955 Bill shelved as a result of opposition within the ruling party failed to yield any surplus land because the ceiling was envisaged on the basis of individual ownership. It subsequently modified in 1971 by an ordinance. In 1973 a further amendment was enacted and the ceiling was made conditional on the basis of treating the family as a unit. The report on agricultural census 1970-71. Bihar reported that or nearly 9000 acre accruing from the implementation of the Act is indeed an achievement. There can be no greater proof of ineffectiveness than this. There were other legislations, viz.the Bihar Land Reforms (Amendment)Bill 1970, the Bihar Public Land Encroachement (Amendment) ordinance and the Bihar privileged persons Homestead Tenancy (Amendment)Bill. All of these were designed to acquire surplus land. For example the Bihar Public Land Reforms ordinance sought to acquire Government land for the landless. But it could achieve very little because most of the Government land had already been encroached upon by the dominant land holders who would not allow possession of the land by the landless in case it was made over to them. To the Bihar privileged persons Homestead Tenancy Bill, the land holders replied by resisting to large scale evictions. Doreen Warriner (1969:141) has remarked in this context "the cycling laws were meant to achieve two objective at the same time. They were meant, first of all, to reduce the holding of the large land owners and secondly to redistribute the surplus recovered from them among the poor and the landless. It is widely admitted that the Government measures designed to achieve these objectives have failed",. Andre Beteille (1969 : 31) has also keep the same view that, "There has been wide spread evasion of the ceiling law so that not much surplus land could be recovered. The little that was recovered has not been redistributed in satisfactory way because of administrative bottle necks which have acted to the advantage of the higher strata and to the detriment of the lower." The Commissioner of Scheduled Castes and Scheduled Tribes, Dr. Brahmdeo Sharma, has also pointed out this fact in his 28th report presented to be president of India on 31.10.1989. He pointed that land lordism should be ended. Land should be to Tillers. Commissioner has observed that land lordism in rural areas is developing. The rural labourers are in plight. Commissioner has also suggested in his report that there should be minimum wages for all. It is a very bad thing that the farm labourers are paid very low wages whereas factory labourers are paid much. This thing is against the tenants of Indian constituation. The commissioner has suggested the new and effective land reform law.

"Kisan lobbies, and leftist forces are also demanding ownership of land for the tiller and actively helping in the enforcement of Bataidari and other progressive land legislations. Bihar is an extreme case but the basic imbalance is common enough.The demand for the pittance stipulated under the minium wages act is rejected as insolence militancy is reinforced initiative. S.K.Dutta Ray 1980 in his article "Harijan on the march' pointed out that the Harijans of Bihar are most aggressive and bloody is for economic reason. S.K.Dutta Ray has quoted"... They are not aggressively on the March in Bihar, because, as Dr.Jagarnath Mishra Former Chief Minister of Bihar and economist too) once put as there are only two classes in his state (Bihar) the landed and the landless. Blood is split whenever the latter demands what that former refuses to yield. "(Sunanda K.Dutta Ray: 1980). Even though the Harijan formerly received land under redistribution schemes (Ceiling land or Bhootan land) they are seldom allowed to enjoy it, landless people specially Harijans and Adivasis are in danger of assault by the landlords.The seventies saw the birth of land grab agitation in Bihar. Different political parties were involved in the agitation. But it seems that that agitation owning to its diffuse character proved ineffective. It is about the same time in the later part of the sixties and the beginning of the seventies that Naxal activities were started in Bihar." S.K. Dutta Ray (1980) also shows the existence of tension and conflict on Naxal ground. "Little wonder that Naxalite violence gripped 14 Bihar districts in middle seventies or till now.The activists were not interested in the Marxist Leninist, Elysian they were anxious to settle old scores with tyrannic landlords who encroached on Khas Mahal Land, exacted virtually free, labour and insisted on bounded, service heeded by slogans of 'Land to the Tiller' whetted appetites without satisfying them."

In all parts of the country agrarian society has been for centuries graded into layers or strata which were hierarchically arranged. These layers might not all be present in one local community. In some areas there might be many layers and in other's only a few one or other of the strata might be internally differentiated at one place and relatively homogeneous at another. In other words, the pattern was every where hierarchical although the details of the hierarchy and the extent to which it was elaborated varied greatly in both space and time. This strata may be said as inequality. In equality can be studied not fully as a mode of existence but also as a mode of consciousness. (Beteille:1969:14). The exstence of inequality in any way creates tension and conflict in any form of society may that society be traditional one.

In the traditional social and cultural milien, in which the dependence of a labourer was in extricably tied up with his low caste and depressed economic status, the servility of the laboures in relation to his malik (master) was the norm. In the changed enviroument when a low caste and down trodden labourer questions the wages given to him and demands more favourable terms of work, he is calling into question the entire frame work of dependence and subjection which informs the Malik's perception of the relationship. The tension inherent in such a situation attains an explosive dimension when the desperate labourers try to advance their demands further through organisation. It is in this procese that the labourers in various parts of Bihar have became involved with political groups and organisations. In response the maliks are indulging in organised burning, looting and killing as reprisals.

Even though the Maliks have resorted to such drastic reprisals against the effort of the labourers to better their working conditions. There appears to be a fundamental misrepresentation of the basic issues, both in governement circle and in the mass media. In fact there is a tendency to rationalise such events simply as 'Atrocities against Harijans or Tribes.'But the main component in this pattern is ralationship between Malik and the agricultural labourers.

With the abolition of zamindari and the enactment of protective legislation, the landowners have formed new forms of labour relations to continue their hold on labour whild remaining within the confines of the law. This is for instance, in Bihar, is the case of labourers like the halwaha (ploughman) and charwaha (Those who graze cattle). In eddition to daily wages, the landlords give them a small piece of land to build their dwellings and for cultivation for personal consumption these labourers are formarly hired annually on a contract basis though in practice they continue to be attached to the landlord from generation to generation the annual contract saves the landlords from the provision of protective legisation which would otehrwise have made these labourers the owners of the land they have been liking on and tilling. Since they do not even own the land on which they build their houses they are dependent on the landlord, thus making it difficult for they to be assrtive.

The number of such labourers is small. The majority of the labourers are choota or casual labourers. They are not directly dependent on the landlord. But as we see this is not free labour in the modern sense of the term. Scarcity of alternative employment indebtedness and payment in kind have made this casual labour in essence a subjucated labour. Now the cost of the basic necesities of life have raised, it is simply the need for survial which has regulated in the demand for increasing the wages and therefore, the organisation of the agricultural labour. This organisation has made the labourers conscious for their actual rights is relation to minimum wages. The labourers in some parts of Bihar are no more readly to be exploited in relation to minimum wages.

This minimum wages has turned many parts of Bihar in tensed condition between agricultural labourer and land lords. In context of minimum wages it is very pertinent to write here that Utter Pradesh has developed enough due to green revolution and proper facilities by the state government. The land lords of these are as are paying the agriculture labourers more than minimum wages. Due to proper facilities of comunication agricultural labourers of Bihar use to go these developed areas as for earning more money. When they return from there they ask the same rate of wages in Bihar, where as due to unscientific cultivation cultivators or, landlords are unable to pay the minimum wages to agricultural labourers which has been (fixed not on regional and productive basis). This situation compelled the land lords and agricultural labourers in tensed situation.

Noted social thinker B. Kuppuswamy(1972:76) has also realised the role of economic factors in the creation and exacerbation of social tension particularly in rural areas. Lack of capital influences the situation and threatens in increase social tension in rural areas.

J.M.Simie has also remarked that "the distribution of resources such as property, wealth and special skills determines the structure of society..its underlying distribution of resources and the different interest of groups found in different parts of social structure. They exist in a conteneous state of dynamic tension in which different groups seeking to further their interests..."

As it has been observed that the basis of caste carnage that often took place in some of the villages in our country most of them are economic in nature. The landless people feel themselves being exploited by the land owners. They are forced to work in the fields of economically sound persons on returns of petty loans. They are foced to work in the fields of economically sound persons without paying minimum wages fixed by the Government. In Bihar instances mentioned above can be easily seen. Bataidari system (share crops harvesting) has been implemented by the Bihar Government but Bataidars are seldom paid as per Bataidari law by the economically sound person. The land reform has been implemented but still land is in the hands of economically sound persons. The land acquired in Bhoodan movement was distributed among downtrodden but those lands have been grabbed by the economically sound persons. This thing created choas among landless and gradually consciousness developed among landless. They have become violent against economically sound persons. Violent way of demanding generates violence for implementing Bataidari Act and other land reform measures like distribution of Bhoodan lands and Khas Mahal lands. The shameful Parasbigha (A village of Bihar State), the village which become the scence of gruesome caste violence early in February, 1980 is situated to the right of the Jehandabad Gaya Road, some 5 Kms.from the sub-divisional head quarters of Jehanabad in the state of Bihar. From the road to the village, a distance of about two kilometers has to be covered through paddy fields before one is able to reach the village. During rainy season, the undulating foot-paths in between the fields becomes solemnly, extremely narrow and untracesible.

It was this village that was invaded by a pack of upper caste Bhumihars in the night of February, 6, 1980. Houses were set on fire and when the inmates tried to escape, they were shot and thrown into the leaping flames. Twelve lives were lost, 7 women, 2 children and 3 men of them, six alone belonged to the family of Sukhdeo Bhagat, a shepherd by caste. The Bhumihars were revenging the murder of Niranjan Sharma, one of their caste who was assassinated in October, 1979 in the village. The Parasbigha tragedy sprang out of some of the landed conflict. The main cause behind this carnage was Khas Mahal Land. The landlords captured the 52 Acres of Khas Mahal Land which the Harijans were willing to have. Polarisation of the entire village between two warring factions, one led by Sharma, the major land owner and other led by Sukhdeo Bhagar, shepherd schoolteacher seems to give it a colour of a struggle between the deprive and the deprived.

In Pipra village the violence and conflict which took place in February 25, 1980 was also related to class tension. The play behind the curtain in Pipra was wage, desrupted sex and rural conflict, caste gang, linkage with the Naxals, and the land grabbing.

In Barai village which is situated in Monghyr district of Tarapur P.S. (Bihar State) the caste carnage between Harijans and Yadav caste was related to land. On 11 October in broad day light, a group of Yadava community attacked the Harijan's huts of Barai village. The havoc was created. Two persons were killed and all the Harijans of this village left the village and came to Tarapur police station. The cause of this carnage was the Bhoodan land of this village. Bhoodan land was distributed among Harijans in 1951. Harijans captured the land and started cultivation on Co-operative basis. But the dominant caste Yadavas were in no mood to compromise with the acts. Harijans resisted and the conflict arose in this village.

On March 28, 1991 former Primer Minister Rajiv Gandhi visited Rajpur and Rampur villages of Madhepura district (Bihar State). In this village a caste carnage took place which invited Rajiv Gandhi to visit this village (As per 29 March 1991 Hindustan report). The pramukh of this village, Sri Shyam Deo Yadav, attacked Harijan Tola with four to five thousand muslemen. The Harijans of this village, under the leadership of leftist force or I.P.F. leader, had built huts on the 25 Bihga Gair Majura land. This land was under the custody of Sri Shyamdeo Yadav. He did not accept the acts of Harijan so he with his armed militia attacked Harijans. So the nature of this caste earnage or Harijan atrocities is economic in nature. Similar situation is prevailing in may villages of Bihar. In Balia, Bargoan (Saharsa district), Sukhsena, Chandwa (Purnea district), Parwaha (Araria district) tension and conflict is prevailing. In Bargoan, Sukhsena, Parwaha, Chandwa the Advasis (Santhal) have capatured the Bataidari land. Santhals are not giving any crops to land owners. Santhal used to say 'Land is to tiller'. Land owners are grouping against Santhal militants. In 1971, in the month of December, handreds of Santhal's huts were burnt in Chandwa village, About 200 Santhals were killed. The cause of this carrage was the land grabbing. In 80s in Kopa village, Madhepura District (Bihar State) four Harijans were killed by the gunmen of Kopa Mahanth. In this village District Administration Distributed the surplus land of Kopa Mahanth, Late Sunder Giri, among landless Harijans. Harijans captured those lands but Mahanth was resisting and went to high Court in protest.The situation took that turn that conflict are between Mahanth and Harijans. Kopa Mahanth was killed. Tension is still prevailing in this villagae due to land.

In some parts of rural area minimum wages in one of the important causes of rural tension. Due to consciousness agricultural labourer demanding the minimum wages fixed by government or the minimum wages as paid by in many parts of developed agricultural areas. The farmers do not want to pay. In this situation there tension between financial agricultural labourers.

A Chauri village (Bihar) in 1972 the landless (Scheduled-caste) and the landlords got locked into the dispute over the scale of wages. The land lord approched the police and passed on the names of those who were in the forefront of the wage demand. Although not directly concerved. The police obliged their by taking a partisam view of situation. But the situation took an unexpected turn. The Scheduled caste, landless, inspired by the justness of their cause, registed the police as also the police attempt to arrest the opinion leaders. As the subsequent official report shouwed. The police had to open fire to control the unruly and stone throwing mob. As a result, four persons died on the spot and 24 others sustained gun shot injuries thus due to wage Chauri village remained tensed since long.

In Marmadiri (Bihar) Landlords of the village killed dalit agricultural labour on March 16th 1980.

In April 1980, Bishenpur Sarnia, Bihar a local landlord of the village Deoria Kothi, Para-block, Muzaffarpur District, was released on bail after six months of imprisonment. He was sent to jail as accused in the murder of a peasent leader. He came back to the village to take revenge on the followers of the local peasent organisation. He and his men killed two activisits, Raghubans Ray and Bainath Ray, Bainath Ray was the Sarpanch of the village.

At Kerserwa (Bihar) on June 29th 1980 a large army of landlords,their musclemen and police, numbering about 500, surrounded the village Kerserwa, Rohtas District. They seized the village for over eighteen hours in search of an alleged dacoit Mohan Bhind. Unable to find him , they picked up four young dalits, tied them up and rode horses over their chests and killed them.

In Gua (Bihar) on September 8th. 1980 a group of Adivasi assembled at Gua, a small mini town in Singbhum district. They had gathered for a demonstration which was to end up presenting a memorandum to the local police and forest officials. The Bihar Military police opened fire on this peaceful gathering and three adivasis were killed on the spot and a number of others injured. The injured were taken to the near by TISCO hospital. As soon as the first batch of nine adivasis were brought to the hospital, they were surrounded by the armed police who opened fire once again. This time 9 people were killed.

At Shankarpur (Bihar) Dispute over the settlement of Government land led to an attack on the Harijan Basti of the village Shankarpur, Araria District. On the November 1980, their houses were set on fire in which an 8 year old girl was burn to death.

At Baipi (Bihar) on Novemeber 24th, 1980, armed police raided the village Baipi, Chakradharpur Block, Singbhum district in search of an adivasi activisit, Suniya Joja. Unable to find him, the police misbehaved with his wife against which the gathered villagers protested. In a fit of anger police opened fire as a result of which an adivasi Tikud laguri, was killed.

At Bairiganj in late December, Dhanraj, a blindman, was shot dead by armedmen of Bhumisena, in Bairiganj Punpun block, Patna District.He was going to Malikpur to arbitrate in an agrarian dispute. Dhanraj was well known in has locality as a poet.

At Birampur (Bihar) since the mid-seventies, an agitation was going on in the village Birampur, Arrah block, Bhojpur districts, against the local Zamindar on various issues, sometimes back. The villagers took possession of some gain Mazurna land and setup their huts there. The Zamindr and his men since then have been harassing them in many ways and they filed a case against the Harijans. But the Harijans won the case.Soon after on 26 June, an armed party of the Zamindar and his men attacked the Harijan Basti and set fire to four hunts. They were joined by the armed police from the local camp. One person,Shyam Dayal was killed.

At Siswa (Bihar) on Agust 26th 1981 a 14 year old Harijan boy, Gujjan Ram was beaten to death by the police at siswa village in East Champarn district. It was done by the police on the provocation of landlords.

At Maithila (Bihar) on September 17th 1981, three local peasent activists were arrested by the police who claimed that they were Naxalites' and were carrying, inflarmmatory material'. They were beaten with lathis and were later shot dead, in the village maithila, Maner block, Bhojpur district.In Patna (Bihar) the growing conflict between the landlords and the poor and landless; peasents led by the Kisan Sabha become intensified in different blocks of Patna district in late October. On October 30th 1981, senior police officials at the area led over a hundred men of Bihar military police in Massive raids throughout the affected blocks. In a span of a week from then the armed policemen shot killed surinder Mehta and Chandravati of Narihi Pirihi villages in Beshinarpur block, Devinder Ram of Kajra village, Devaki Manjhi and Jankie Manjhi at Bahuara village both from Naubalpur block Devinder Ramdas of Beshinarpur village in Masauri block and Laxman Choudry of Parh Bigha village in Dhavrwa block. In all seven people were killed including a 15 year old newely married girl.

At Barsoi (Bihar) on November 19th 1981, police opened fire on a demonstration out side the Barsoi police station, Katihar district, four nexalites were killed.

At Sarjomhatu (Bihar on November 25th 1981. a police party led by the D.S.P. went to Sarjomhatu village, Sonwa block, Singhbhum district, to arrest some tribals involved in a case of forest felling.They destroyed the houses of the wanted villagers. When the villagers protested. They opend fire, killing Tepa Hembrom, a 19 years old tribal.

At Mjhauli (Bihar) the village Majhamli, Gaya District, was attacked by the land lords on 18th March 1982. The attackers set fire to the house of on activisit of the peasant movement, Bijay Chaudary, who was burnt to death. Chaudary was a blind man.

At Mahadiput (Bihar)on March 20th 1982, in the village Mahadipur, Patna District, Dahuram, a Kisan Sabha activisit was killed by the land lords in the early morning house while he was going to his masoor fields. At Baluaha (Bihar). Conflict between peasents and land lords has been brewing in and around Baluaha village, Rajnagar Block, Madhukari district. Since early 1982,when more than twenty share croppers filed a claimant suit in the court. On 2 April on altercation took, place between chanaiya Mandal a share cropper and the landlord. Sukhdev Thankur, a carpenter of the village, intervened on behalf of Mandal. Police who were present all throughout the incident intervened at that stage and beat him up severely and he was dragged to a landlord's house and was forced to drink urine as a result of which his condition deteriorated and he was taken to madhubari hospital were he died. Next day, on April 3rd, 1982 about 500 villagers demonstrated at the land lords house in protest police opened fire on the gathering, killing six people (Unofficial estimates eight) on the sport.

Adivasis of Chaibasa, Singhbhum district have been agitating against the construction of Kuju Dam, which will submerge their villages. The dam is part of the multipurpose subernrekha valley project. They have been agitating under the leadership of Kadkai Dan Sangrash Samiti. In the early house of April 4th 1982 a police part, led by local D.S.P. raided Illigara village and took away Gangaram Kolundia Gangaram 40, a retired Naib subedar of Indian Army, was tortured to death. He was the general secretary of Kadkai Dan Sangarsh Samiti.

At Bira (Bihar) on April 25th 1982, armed landlords attacked the village Bira,Ghosi block,Gaya district.The village was one of the strongholds of local peasant organisation.They entered at the dead of the night and began setting fire to the houses in the tola of Mushars. As the villagers woke up began to run in pamic, the land lords fired at them. Three old women Bhatami Devi (80) Mhagi Devi (80) and Bhagiya Devi (60) one young boy Ram Bhajan Manjhi (15) and a young girl Pipariya (12) were killed.

At Deoramath (Bihar) on May 1st 1982, three alleged Naxalites, including a woman, was killed in an encounter with the police in

Deoramnath village, Ghosi block, Gaya district.

At Mohammadpur (Bihar) on May 4th 1982 a group of landlords killed an alleged Naxalite at Mahammadpur village, Punpun block, Patna district.

At Chhapang Bigha (Bihar) Bhumisena landlords attacked the village Chhapang Bigha, Masauri block, Patna District. All the Harijan families left the village. Ganesh Mistry a Young activist who refused to leave in defince, was killed.

At Bara (Bihar) in the village Bara, Masuari block, Patna district, a Young kissan Sabha follower Sudeshan, was killed by the five land owners.

At Kakoje (Bihar) a three hundred strong armed police force entered Kakoji village Gaya district and raided the houses of Harijans. Three peasant activists were captured and shot dead.

At Gaini (Bihar) a Militant movement of landless labourers resulted in intense conflict between the landlords and the landless labourers in parts of Aurangabad district in early 1982. On June 27th a mob led by landlords attacked the Dalit basti in Gaini village. Seven People were killed.

At Jamuk (Bihar) in Jank Jehanabad block, Gaya district a procession of land less labourers, led by the Majdoor Kisan Sagram Samiti, was attacked by armed landlords in presence of the police on July 2nd. Two Dalit agricultural labourers siddeshwar Machi and Sheo Pujan Paswan were killed on the spot.

At Kadirchak,(Bihar) on July 3rd 1982,Gyanchand Bhagat.A small peasent was killed by the landlords in Kadirchak village, Jehanabad block, Gaya district. Bhagat was an activist of Majdoor Kisan Sangarsh Samiti.

At Bhagwanpur (Bihar) a gang of Landowners, armed with rifles and guns attacked the village Bhagwanpur, Jehanabad block. Gaya district, on August 10th, 1982. They kidnapped three activists of Majdoor kisan Sangarash Sammiti. Later all the three of them Lakshan Manjhi (20) Sudesh Manjhi (19) and Bal Kishore Manihi (15) were tortured to death. All of them come from Dalit landless families.

At Tarari (Bihar) five extremists were killed by the farmers in Tarari village, Konch block, Gaya district on August 18th 1982.

At Ichagarh (Bihar) in October people of the Ichagarh block began an agitation demanding the declaration of the area as a drought affected area. On 21 October, about 500 people under the leadership of Krantikari Chatrajuva Morch, demonstrated out side the Inchagarh Block, Office. Police opened fire on the the demonstration killing two people. Ajit Mahato and Dananjoy Mahato. Both of them were student leaders of the area.

At Palajori (Bihar) people in Palajori development block, of Santhal Paraganas have been agitating for the implementation and extension of varous welfare schemes, on 7th October a group of people, led by 14 out of 17 Mukhiyas of the block, demonstrated of the office of the Block Development Officer. Police opened fire on the demonstrators. Four people (Unofficial estimates seven) were killed.

At Goghi Bariarpur (Bihar) agitation for ligher wages picked up in and Aroung goghi Bariarpur village, Suryagarha block of Monghyr district in late 1982. In December the labours forcibly harvested the landlords land. On December 25th 1982, police arrested the leader of the organisation Ramashish and 80 others. The villagers immediately demonstrated at the local police station, demanding the release of the arrested persons. The police agreed to do so if the landlord had no objection. The people then proceeded to the landlords house and demonstrated there. The landlord, fired nine rounds at the people, killing four Young men. The landlord, Chandrika Singh was secretary of the Suryagarha block, congress (1) committee.

At Bhavanichal (Bihar) in early January, Nathuna Singh, a small peasant and an activist of Majdoor kisan sangram samiti, was killed by landlords in Bhavarichak, Jehanabad block, Gaya district.

At Barai (Bihar) two naxalite leaders were killed in an encounter with the people in Barai village near Monghyr town in the first week of February 1983.

At Chaurasi (Bihar) Jeydhrath Sharma, a CPI (M) peasant leader, was killed by the goondas of a Zamindar in Chaurasi village, Madhepura district, in early March.

At Surangpur (Bihar) two sympathisers of Majdoor Kisan Sangersh Samiti were killed by the landlords on April 14th 1983 at Bhavanichak. Both of them Rohan Paswan, a teacher and Sheo Dayal Paswan, a small peasant were from Surangpur, Jehanabad block, Gaya district.

At Parthu (Bihar) two Dalit agricultural labourers of Parthu village, Patna district were killed by armed men of Bhumisena in early May. Both of them were associated with Kisan Sabha.

At Tulsichak (Bihar) one dalit agricultural labourer of Tulsichak village. Patna district was killed by armed men of Bhumisena in early May. He was an activist of Kisan Sabha.

At Shahpur (Bihar) Supan Yadav of Chatki village in Bhojpur district was killed in the police lockup in Shahpur on May 2nd 1983. Yadav was a landless labourer associated with local peasant organisation.

At Pataria (Bihar) on the night of May 8th 1983, a van load of a senior police and administrative officials surrounded the village pataria, Jehanabad block, Gaya district. Pataria is one of the holds of local peasant organisation. They raided and searched all the houses of the village. At down a Young activist Pradeep Bhind, was picked up and was interrogated. After the interrogation was over, he was asked to go home, As he turned his back, he was shot dead.

At Panpania (Bihar) Police opened fire on a demonstration of peasants in panpania, Gaya district on May 10th 1983. Five agricultural labourers were killed.

At Gonsa (Bihar) Inderdev Mochi is a 30 year old Dalit landless labourer and an activist of the Kisan Sangarsh Samiti from the villagae Gonsa, Jehanabad block, Gaya district. On May 10th 1983, Six Rajput youths armed with rifles came to the village and shot him dead in the premises of his employer's house. His employer is an additional district magistrate of Bihar state.

At Pahara Pahadia (Bihar) a 'Naxalite' was killed in Pahara Phadia village, Palamu district, in an encoutner'with police in first week of June 1983.

At Gua (Bihar) Adivasi youths of the Chaibasa region have been agitating against un imployment is Singhbhum district. On June 22th

1983, Five of them went to meet the officials at Gua, to submit a memorandum. They were arrested by the police. Later they were tied with ropes to the rear of a police jeep and were dragged by the running jeep for over two hundred metres. Later at the market place, they were hung upside down to a beam put across two poles. Then a police squad flogged them continously. One of them, Vedor Nag Munga, died on the spot. Munga an adivasi was a retired army jawan who took part in Bangla Desh war.

In Patna (Bihar) Shri Kishore Kunal, Senor superintendent of Police, Patna district, which distributing cash compensation for those killed in agrarian disputes, disclosed that 50 Harijan agricultural labourers were killed by landlords in 1982-1983 in Patna district. The situation of killing labourer on the name of naxalite and other is continued in Bihar. In some place some labourers are also killing land lords. There is open fight between two.

Several private sena (armies) has grown all over Bihar as landlords try to protect their holdings. Among them are the Ranbir Sena, the sunlight sena, the Dimound sena, the Brahmrishi sena, the Azad sena, and the Lorik sena.These sena have open fight to Naxals.

The banned Ranbir sena emerged as the most dreaded of the private armies following the massacre of 19 Naxlite supported people at Bathani Tola settlement in Bhojpur district of Bihar in July 1996 and the March 23 killing of 10 villagers of Hawaspur Musharitola in Patna district of Bihar. The Ranbir sena struck again on April 11, 1997 when it butchered eight CPI(ML) sympathisers in Ekwari village in Bhojpur district of Bihar.

The Naxlites extracted its revenge from Ranbir sena in Raghopur village near Patna on Aprial 20, 1997. The blow up of the houses of Janardan Sharma (M.L.A) after dragging out his cousin and five others and shooting them. It is said that this revenge was because Sharma had been linked to the Hawaspur killing .

The state government's standard reaction to the killings seemed to be limited to announcing cash relief to the victims's families. But politicians, cutting across party lines, got the rap when, following the Bathani Tola Massacre, the union government set up a three-men committee to prepare a report on the activities of the Naxal outfits and the private armies. The report pointed out that politicians of various hues were protecting the private armies and the Naxal out fits.

Plagued by criticism the state government launched a grandiose plan'operation Sidharth' to root out the causes for clashes predictably, the special package, involving over 70 crores and aimed at bringing the down trodden to to the mainstream, flopped. The all weather roads linking remote villages and the infrastructure for better communication facilities never came up. The Jawahar Rojgar Yogna replaced the special package, but even its assured income generating schemes failed to curb the Naxalite menace. Gradually leftist or so called Naxalite effect is increasing in whole of Bihar.

As regards tension on economic basis in the area understudy is concerned, Bihara village is interwoven with composite caste. In Nov. 1978 a carnage took place in this village.The Bhoodan land was donated in 1951 by land owners. These lands were distributed among Harijans and Santhals on papers. But the former land owners remained in actual possession of those lands, due to lack of consciousness among Harijans and Santhals. They tilled lands as Batidars of those Bhoodani land. Late Mr. Janardan Pandeya and village head Late Kumar Singh a leftist leader, of Bihara village aroused consciousness among, Harijans and Santhals. After 1977 the Harijans and Santhals Bataidar refused to pay crops of those Bhoodani land to the so called old land owners. In this way tensions prevailed and huts of Harijans and santhals were burnt by the Gunmen of old land owner of Bhumihar caste. Ten persons of Harijans and Santhals were killed. In July 1995 Kumar Singh has also been killed. Till now this village is tense due to land.

Due to consciousness among labourers they started to ask for the minimum wages. The landlords of this village do not want to give minimum wages to labourers. On several occasions labourers of this village have made strike (Hartal). Sometime, they have started to migrate from their village to Punjab, Haryana, Delhi in search of proper wages. The land owners of this village is mostly of Bhumihar caste (Forward caste) and labourers are of low caste or backward caste. The fight of land lords and landless labourers of Bataidars has taken the shape of the fight between forward caste and Backward caste. Mostly Backward Caste of this village are backing harijans and santhals. But open fight is between landless and landlords.

Data has been collected from this very Bihara village to ascertain how economy creates social tension. On the basis of Schedule data has been presented in Tabular form on consecutive pages.

Table -1 (A) Basis Caste Gr.

Frequency/-%
No./200

SL.No.	Caste Gr. No of respondents	A Is there discrimination of high and low on the economic basis.		B Is there any organization on the basis of economically high and low.	
		Yes	**No.**	**Yes**	**No.**
1.	F.C.Hindu & Muslim 96	96/100	0	96/100	0
2.	B.C.Hindu & Muslim 56	56/100	0	56/100	0
3.	Low Caste/48 (Harijan and Adivasi)	48/100	0	48/100	0
	Total - 200	**200/100**	**0**	**200/100**	**0**

Table -1 (B) Basis occupation Gr.

Frequency-%
No. 200

SL.No.	Occupation Gr. No of respondents	A Is there discrimination of high and low on the economic basis.		B Is there any organization on the basis of economically high and low.	
		Yes	**No.**	**Yes**	**No.**
1.	Labour/70	70/100	0	70/100	0
2.	Caste occupation/12	12/100	0	12/100	0
3.	Business/2	2/100	0	2/100	0
4.	Service/32	32/100	0	32/100	0
5.	Independent Occupation/4	4/100	0	4/100	0
6.	Agriculture/80	80/100	0	200/100	0
	Total -200	**200/100**	**0**	**200/100m**	**0**

Table No. 1 (C) Basis literacy gr.

Frequency-%
No. 200

SL.No.	Literacy Gr. No of respondents	A Is there discrimination of high and low on the economic basis.		B Is there any organization on the basis of economically high and low.	
		Yes	No.	Yes	No.
1.	Illiterate/110	110/100	0	110/100	0
2.	Middle range educated/36	36/100	0	36/100	0
3.	High range educated/54	200/100	0	200/100	0
,	**Total -200**	**200/100**	**0**	**200/1C0**	**0**

Table - 1 (D) Basis Age gr.

Frequency-%
No. 200

SL.No.	Age Gr. No of respondents	A Is there discrimination of high and low on the economic basis.		B Is there any organization on the basis of economically high and low.	
		Yes	No.	Yes	No.
1.	Upto 30 years/40	40/100	0	40/100	0
2.	31 Yrs. to 50 yrs/100	100/100	0	100/100	0
3.	More than 53 Yrs/60	60/100	0	60/100	0
	Total -200	**200/100**	**0**	**200/100**	**0**

(Note: Here in all tables F means frequency, N means, gr. means group F.C. means Forward Caste; B.C. means Backward Caste)

Table No. 1 (A), 1 (B), 1 (C), and 1(D) indicates that 100 respondents of each caste gr. occupation gr, literacy gr. and age gr. of the total no. of the respondents have reported that there is discrimination of high and low on the economic basis and there is organization on the basis of economically high and low. None of the respondents has reported in negative about these question.

Table - 2 (A) Basis Caste gr.

Frequency-%

No. 200

SL.No.	Caste Gr.	A		B	
	No of respondents	Whether you attend the ceremoney of wealthier person as brotherly		Whether you feel social distance on the basis of economic high and low.	
		Yes	**No.**	**Yes**	**No.**
1.	F.C. Hindu & Muslim/96	89/92.71	7/7.29	51/53.13	45/46.87
2.	B.C. Hindu & Muslim/56	0	56/100	56/100	0
3.	Low Caste/48	0	48/100	48/100	0
	Total -200	**89/44.5**	**111/55.5**	**155/77.5**	**45/22.5**

Table - 2 (B) Basis Occupation gr.

Frequency-%

No. 200

SL.No.	Occupation Gr.	A		B	
	No of respondents	Whether you attend the ceremony of wealthier person as brotherly		Whether you feel social distance on the basis of economic high and low.	
		Yes	**No.**	**Yes**	**No.**
1.	Labour/70	0	70/100	70/100	0
2.	Caste occupation/12	2/16.67	10/83.33	12/100	0
3.	Business/2	2/100	0	1/50	1/50
4.	Service/32	26/81.25	6/18.75	16/50	16/50
5.	Independent occupation/80	4/100	0	2/50	2/50
6.	Agriculture/80	55/68.75	25/31.25	34/67.5	26/32.5
	Total -200	**89/44.5**	**111/55.5**	**155/77.5**	**45/22.5**

Table - 2 (C) Basis literacy gr.

Frequency-%
No. 200

SL.No.	Literacy Gr. No of respondents	A Whether you attend the ceremony of wealthier person as brotherly.		B Whether you feel social distance on the basis of economic high and low.	
		Yes	**No.**	**Yes**	**No.**
1.	Illiterate/110	30/27.27	80/72.73	105/95.46	5/4.45
2.	Middle range educated/36	15/41.67	21/59.33	25/69.44	11/30.56
3.	High range educated/54	44/81.48	10.18.52	25/46.30	29/53.70
	Total -200	**89/44.5**	**111/55.5**	**155/77.5**	**45/22.5**

Table - 2 (D) Basis Age gr.

Frequency-%
No. 200

SL.No.	Age Gr. No of respondents	A Whether you attend the ceremony of wealthier person as brotherly.		B Whether you feel social distance on the basis of economic high and low.	
		Yes	**No.**	**Yes**	**No.**
1.	Upto 30 yrs/40	16/40	24/60	38/95	2/5
2.	31yrs to 50 yrs/100	43/43	57/57	81/81	19/19
3.	More than 51 yrs/60	30/50	30/50	36/60	24/41
	Total -200	**89/44.5**	**111/55.5**	**155/77.5**	**45/22.5**

Table -2 (A) indicate that 92.71% forward caste respondents of the total number of the respondents have reported that they attend the ceremony of wealthier person as friendly other than this 7.29% forward caste, 100% Backward caste, 1000% low caste of the total number of the respondents have reported that they do not attend the ceremony of wealthier persons brotherly in part 'A' of this table. In part 'B' of table number 2 (A) only 46.87% forward caste of the total number of the respondents do not feel social distance on the basis of economic "high and low" on the other hand 33.13% forward caste 100% Backward caste, 100% low caste of the total number of the respondents feel social distance on the basis of economically high and low.

Table number 2 (B) indicates that 16.67% caste occupants, 100% businessmen, 81.25% servicemen, 100% independent occupants, 68.75% agriculturist of the total number of the respondents have reported that they attend the ceremony of wealthier person on friendly terms. 100% labourers, 83.33% caste occupants, 18.75% servicemen, 31.25% agriculturist of the total number of the respondents have reported that they do not attend ceremony of wealthier persons as brotherly. In part 'B' of this table 100% labourers, 100% caste occupants, 50% businessmen, 50% servicemen, 50% independent occupants, 87.5% agriculturists of the total number of the respondents have reported that they feel social distance on the basis of economically high and low.

Table Number 2 (C) indicates that 27.27% illiterate, 41.67% middle range educated, 81.48% high range educated respondents of the total number of the respondents have reported they attend the ceremony of wealthier person as brotherly. 72.73 illiterates, 58.53% Middle range educated, 18.5% high range educated respondents of the total number of the respondents have reported that they do not attend the ceremony of wealthier person as brotherly. In part 'B' of this table 95.46% illiterate, 69.44% middle range educated, 46.6% high range educated respondents of the total number of the respondents have reported that they feel social distance on the basis of economically high and low. Rest of the respondents do not feel any social distance.

Table number 2(D) indicate that 40% upto age of 30 years, 3% 31 years to 50% more than 51 years of the total number of the respondents have reported that they attend the ceremony of wealthier persons as brotherly. 60% upto age of 30 years, 57% 31 years to 50% years 50% more than 51 years of the total number of the respondents have reported that they do not attend the ceremony of wealthier person as brotherly. Part 'B' of this table indicates that 95% upto age of 30 years, 81% 31 years to 50 years, 60% more than 51 years of the total number of the respondents have reported that they feel social distance on the basis of economically high and low. Rest of the respondents do not feel social distance on economically high and low.

Concluding this table it may be stated that 45.5% of the total number of the respondents attend the ceremony of wealthier persons as brotherly whereas 55.5% respondents of the total number of the respondents do not attend the ceremony of wealthier person as brotherly. High range educated people more attend the ceremony of wealtheir person that of illiterate. There is co-relation between the frequency of attending the ceremony of wealthier person as brotherly and literacy group. There is also the co-relation between the age and the respondents of attending the ceremony of wealthier person as brotherly. Low range group are attending the ceremony of wealthier person in low frequency and high range age group are attending the ceremony of wealthier person in high frequency. As regard social distance on economically high and low. 77.5% of the total number of the respondents have reported that they feel social distance on economically high and low. There is also co-relation betweem literacy and feeling of social distance on economically high and low. Illiterate feel maximum social distance on economically high and low. Just double frequency is seen as regard to illiterate in comparison to high range educated group. These tables indicate that there is social distance on the economically high and low in the area concerned.

Table -3 (A) Basis Caste group

Frequency-%
No. 200

SL.No.	Caste group No of respondents	A Whether land ceiling has been implemented in your village.		B If yes that land has been distributed among land-less and that is in posse-ssion to landless.	
		Yes	**No.**	**Yes**	**No.**
1.	F.C. Hindus & Muslim/96	96/100	0	20/20.83	76/79.17
2.	B.C. Hindu & Muslim/56	56/100	0	0	56/100
3.	Low Caste/48	48/100	0	0	48/100
	Total -200	**200/100**	**0**	**20/10**	**180/90**

Table - 3(A), 3 (B), 3 (C) and 3 (D) has been divided into two parts i.e. 'A' and 'B' in part A of these respondents view has been tabulated whether land ceiling has been implements in their village. Respondents were requested to answer in yes or number In part 'B' of these tables the respondents who answered affirmatively in part 'A' were again asked to answer in yes or number Whether the land acquired in ceiling has been distributed among landless they are in possession to them.

Table - 3 (B) Basis Occupation group

Frequency-%

No. 200

SL.No.	Occupation group	A		B	
	No of respondents	Whether land ceiling has been implemented in your village.		If yes that land has been distributed among land-less and that is in posse-ssion to landless.	
		Yes	No.	Yes	No.
1.	Labour/70	70/100	0	0	70/100
2.	Caste occupation/12	12/100	0	0	12/100
3.	Business/2	2/100	0	0	2/10
4.	Service/32	32/100	0	0	32/100
5.	Independent Occupation/4	4/100	0	0	4/100
6.	Agriculture/80	80/100	0	20/25	60/75
	Total -200	**200/100**	**0**	**20/10**	**180/90**

Table - 3 (C) Basis Literacy group

Frequency-%

No. 200

SL.No.	Literacy group	A		B	
	No of respondents	Whether land ceiling has been implemented in your village.		If yes that land has been distributed among land-less and that is in posse-ssion to landless.	
		Yes	No.	Yes	No.
1.	Illiterate/110	110/100	0	8/7.27	102/92.73
2.	Middle range educated/36	36/100	0	5/13.39	31/86.11
3.	High range educated/54	54/100	0	7/12.96	47/87.04
	Total -200	**200/100**	**0**	**20/10**	**180/90**

Table -3 (A) indicates that 100% respondents of each caste group have reported land ceiling has been implemented. In part 'B' of this table 79.1% forward caste 100% backward caste and 100% low caste respondents of the total number of the respondents. Who answered affirmatively in part 'A' has reported that land acquired in ceiling are not in possession to landless. Only 20.83% forward caste respondents of the total number of the respondents have reported that landless are in possession to ceiling land which was distributed among them.

Table - 3 (D) Basis Age gr.

Frequency-%

No. 200

SL.No.	Age gr. No of respondents	A Where land ceiling has been implemented in your village.		B If yes that land has been distributed among land-less and that is in posse-ssion to landless.	
		Yes	No.	Yes	No.
1.	Upto 30 yrs/40	40/100	0	0	40/100
2.	31 yrs. to 50 yrs/100	0	0	5/5	95/95
3.	More than 51 yrs/60	60/100	0	15/25	45/75
	Total -200	**200/100**	**0**	**20/10**	**180/90**

Table -3 (B) indicates that 100% respondents of each occupation group have reported that land ceiling has been implemented. In part 'B' of this table 25% agriculturists of the total number of the respondents have reported that ceiling land which was distributed among landless are in possession to landless people. Rest of the respondents of each occupation group have reported that those ceiling land are not inpossession tol and less.

Table -3 (C) indicate that 100% respondents of each literacy group have reported that land ceiling has been implemented. In part 'B' of this table 7.27% illiterate, 13.89% of the middle range educated, 12.96% high range educated of the total number of the respondents have reported ceiling land which was distributed among landless are in possession to them. Rest all the respondents of all literacy group have given their answer in negative.

Table -3 (D) indicates that 100% respondents of each age group have reported that ceiling land has been distributed among landless. In part 'B' of this table 5% 31 years to 50 years and 25% more than 51 years of age group of the total number of the respondets have reported the that the ceiling land which was distributed among landless are in possession to them. Rest all the respondets have reported negatively about this question.

Concluding these tables it may be stated that 100% respondents feel that land ceiling has been implemented in the village. 10% respondents of the total number of the respondents have reported that the ceiling land which was distributed among landless are in possession to them. Whereas 90% respondents of the total number of the respondets have reported that the ceiling land which was distributed among landless are not in possession to them.

Table - 4 (A) Basis Caste group.

Frequency-%

No. 200

SL.No.	Caste group	A		B		C	
	No of respondents	Whether Bataidari Kanoon has been implemented in your village.		Whether any conflict has occu-rred on the basis of bataidari Kanoon		Whether there is tension on the basis of bataidari Kanoon	
		Yes	No.	Yes	No.	Yes	No.
1.	F.C. Hindu & Muslim/96	96/100	0	96/100	0	96/100	0
2.	B.C. Hindus & Muslim/56	56/100	0	56/100	0	56/100	0
3.	Low Caste/48	48/100	0	48/100	0	48/100	0
	Total 200	**200/100**	**0**	**200/100**	**0**	**200/100**	**0**

Table - 4 (B) Basis occupation group.

Frequency-%

No. 200

SL.No.	occupation group	A		B		C	
	No of respondents	Whether Bataidari Kanoon has been implemented in your village.		Whether any conflict has occu-rred on the basis of bataidari Kanoon		Whether there is tension on the basis of bataidari Kanoon	
		Yes	No.	Yes	No.	Yes	No.
1.	Labour/70	70/100	0	70/100	0	70/100	0
2.	Cast occupation/12	12/100	0	12/100	0	12/100	0
3.	Bussiness/2	2/100	0	2/100	0	2/100	0
4.	Independent Occupation/4	4/100	0	4/100	0	4/100	0
5.	Service/32	32/100	0	32/100	0	32/100	0
6.	Agriculture/80 80/100	80/100	0	80/100	0	80/100	0
	Total -200	200/100	0	200/100	0	200/100	0

Table - 4 (C) Basis literacy group.

Frequency-%

No. 200

SL.No.	literacy group No of respondents	A Whether Bataidari Kanoon has been implemented in your village.		B Whether any conflict has occu-rred on the basis of bataidari Kanoon		C Whether there is tension on the basis of bataidari Kanoon	
		Yes	No.	Yes	No.	Yes	No.
1.	Illiterate/110	110/100	0	110/100	0	110/100	0
2.	Middle range educated/36	36/100	0	36/100	0	36/100	0
3.	High range educated/54	54/100	0	54/100	0	54/100	0
	Total -200	**200/100**	**0**	**200/100**	**0**	**200/100**	**0**

Table - 4 (D) Basis age group.

Frequency-%

No. 200

SL.No.	age group No of respondents	A Whether Bataidari Kanoon has been implemented in your'village.		B Whether any conflict has occu-rred on the basis of bataidari Kanoon		C Whether there is tension on the basis of bataidari Kanoon	
		Yes	No.	Yes	No.	Yes	No.
1.	Upto 30 yrs/40	40/100	0	40/100	0	40/100	0
2.	31 yrs to 50 yrs /100	100/100	0	100/100	0	100/100	0
3.	More than 52 yrs /60	60/100	0	60/100	0	60/100	0
	Total -200	**200/100**	**0**	**200/100**	**0**	**200/100**	**0**

Note- here Kanoon means law.

Table - 4 (A), 4 (B), 4 (C) and 4 (D) respectively on the basis of caste group occupation gr. literacy gr. and age gr. indicates that 100% respondents have answered that Bataidari Kanoon has been implemented in his village, conflict has occurred on the basis of Bataidari Kanoon and tension is also prevailing due to bataidari kanoorn.

Table -5 (A), 5 (B) and 5 (D) is based on different variables Table number 5 (A) has been divided into three parts i.e,'A','B', and 'C',. Part 'A' of this table indicates that 35.25% F.C. Hindu and Muslim, 10.78 B.C. Hindu and Muslim have reported that village labourers and paid minimum wages prescribed by Government where as on the contrary 68.78 F.C. Hindu and Muslim, 89.22% B.C. Hindu and Muslim 100% Low caste have informed that minimum wages are not paid to village labourers. From this part of the table it is inferred that higher the caste lower the affirmation and lower the caste higher the negation. So 100% respondents of all castes group have informed that strike has held in the village for minimum wages as it has been tabulated in part 'B' of this table, In part of 'C' of this table 100% respondents of all caste group have informed that tension is prevailing in the village due to nonpayment of minimum wages.

Table -5 (B) has been divided into three part i.e. 'A', 'B' and 'C'. In part 'A' of this table 15.62% service holder, 38.75% people engaged in agriculture profession have informed that minimum wages residens have informed that minimum wages is not paid to village labourers. In part 'B' and 'C' of the table 100% respondents of all occupation groups have informed that strike has held in the village for minimum wages and tension is prevailing due to non payment of minimum wages.

Table -5 (C) has been divided into three parts i.e. 'A,'B' and 'C'. Inpart 'A' of this table only 66.67% respondents have informed that minimum prescribed wages fixed by Government is paid to labourers of the village those are the respondents of high range educated. Rest of the respondents have informed that minimum prescribed wages fixed by Government is not paid to village labourers. In part 'B' and 'C' 100% respondents of all literacy group has informed affirmatively of the question concerned.

Table - 5 (D) has been divided into three parts i.e.,'A','B' and 'C'. In part 'A' of this table 100% respondents of 31 years to 51 years age and 53.33% respondents of more than 51 years of age informed that minimum wages prescribed by the Govenment is paid to the labourers of the village. Rest of the respondents have informed negatively in part 'A' of this table. In part 'B' and 'C' of this table all the respondents have informed affirmatively related to the question of part 'B' and 'C' of the table number 5 (C)

Table -5 (A) Basis Caste group.

F/-%

N-200

Sl.No.	Caste group.	A		B		C	
		Whether minimum prescribed wages fixed by Govt. is paid to the village labourers		Whether any strike (hart) in the village has held for minimum wages		Whether any tension is previ-lling in the village due to non payment of minimum wages	
	No of respondents	**Yes**	**No**	**Yes**	**No**	**Yes**	**No**
1.	F. C. Hindus & Muslim /96	30/35.25	66/100	96/100	0	96/100	0
2.	B.C. Hindu & Muslims/56	6/10.78	50/100	56/100	0	56/100	0
3.	Low caste/48	0	48/100	48/100	0	48/100	0
	Total -200	**36/18**	**164/82**	**200/100**	**0**	**200/100**	**0**

Table - 5(D) has been divided into three parts i.e., 'A', B' and 'C'. In part 'A' of this table 100% respondents of 31 years to 51 years of age 53.33% respondents of more than 51 years of age have informed that minimum wages prescribed by the Government is paid to labourers of the village. Rest of the respondents have informed that munimum wages prescribed by the Government is not paid to labourers of the village. In part 'B'and 'C' of this table 100% respondents of all age groups have informed that strike of labourers has held for the minimum wages and tension is ;prevailing due to nonpayment of minimum wages in the village.

Table -5 (B) Basis Occupation group.
Here to write about A,B,C.

F/-%
No.-200

Sl.No.	Occupational group.	A		B		C	
		Whether minimum prescribed wages fixed by Govt. is paid to the village labourers		Whether any strike (harted) in the village has held for minimum wages		Whether any tension is previ-lling in the village due to non payment of minimum wages	
	No of respondents	**Yes**	**No**	**Yes**	**No**	**Yes**	**No**
1.	Labour/70	0	70/100	70/100	0	70/100	0
2.	Caste occupation/12	0	12/100	12/100	0	12/100	0
3.	Business/2	0	2/100	2/100	0	2/100	0
4.	Independence Occupation/4	0	4/100	4/100	0	4/100	0
5.	Service/32	5/15.62	27/84.38	32/100	0	32/100	0
6.	Agriculture/80	31/38.7	49.61.25	80/100	0	80/100	0
	Total -200	**36/18**	**164/82**	**200/100**	**0**	**200/100**	**0**

Table No-5 (C) Basis Literacy group
Here to write about A,B,C

F/-%
NO.-200

Sl. No.	literacy group.	A		B		C	
		Whether minimum prescribed wages fixed by Govt. is paid to the village labourers		Whether any strike (hartal) in the village has held for minimum wages		Whether any tension is previ-lling in the village due to non payment of minimum wages	
	No. Literacy Gr.	**Yes**	**No**	**Yes**	**No**	**Yes**	**No**
1.	Illiterate/110	0	110/100	110/100	0	110/100	0
2.	Middle range educated/36	0	36/100	36/100	0	36/100	0
3.	High range educated/54	36.66.67	18/33.33	54/100	0	54/100	0
	Total -200	**36/18**	**164/82**	**200/100**	**0**	**200/100**	**0**

Table -5(D) Basis Age group.
Here to write about A,B,C

F/-%
N-200

Sl. No.	Age group.	A		B		C	
		Whether minimum prescribed wages fixed by Govt. is paid to the village labourers		Whether any strike (hartal) in the village has held for minimum wages		Whether any tension is previ-lling in the village due to non payment of minimum wages	
	No. of redspondents	**Yes**	**No**	**Yes**	**No**	**Yes**	**No**
1.	Upto 30Yrs /40	0	40/100	40/100	0	40/100	0
2.	31 Yrs to 50 Yrs/100	4/100	96/96	100/100	0	100/100	0
3.	More than 51 Yrs/60	32/53.33	28/46.67	60/100	0	60/100	0
	Total 200	**36/18**	**164/82**	**200/100**	**0**	**200/100**	**0**

Concluding these tables it may concluded that 82% respondents have informed that minimum wages prescribed by the Government is not paid to labourers of the village. 100% respondents have informed respectively that strike has held in the village for minimum wages and tension is prevailing in the village for the nonpayment of minimum wages.

Table No-6 (A) Basis literacy group.

F-%
No-200

Sl.No.	Literacy group.	A		B		C	
		Do you know that Labourers are migrating from your village out side the state for livelihood		Whether labourers migrating due to non payment of minimum wages.		Any govt. organi-sation are making efforts for payment of minimum wages for labourers	
	No of respondents	**Yes**	**No**	**Yes**	**No**	**Yes**	**No**
1.	F.C. Hindu & Muslim/96	96/100	0	66/68.75	30/3.25	30/31.25	66/68.75
2.	B.C. Hindu & Muslim/56	56/100	0	50/89.28	6/10.72	6/10.72	50/89.28
3	Low caste/48	48/100	0	48/100	0	0	48/100
	Total -200	**200/100**	**0**	**164/82**	**36/18**	**36/18**	**164/82**

Table No-6 (B) Basis literacy group.

F-%
No-200

Sl.No.	Occupation group.	A		B		C	
		Do you know that Labourers are migrating from your village out side the state for livelihood		Whether labourers migrating due to non payment of minimum wages.		Any govt. organisation are making efforts for payment of minimum wages for labourers	
	No of respondents	Yes	No	Yes	No	Yes	No
1.	Labour/70	70/100	0	70/100	0	0	70/100
2.	Caste occupation/12	12/100	0	12/100	0	0	12/100
3.	Business/2	2/100	0	2/100	0	0	2/100
4.	Independent Occupation/4	4/100	0	4/100	0	0	4/100
5.	Service/32	32/100	0	27/84.32	5/15.63	5/15.63	27/84.37
4.	Agriculture/80	80/100	0	49/61.25	31/38.75	31/38.75	49/61.25
	Total -200	**200/100**	**0**	**164/82**	**36/18**	**36/18**	**164/82**

Table -6 (C) Basis literacy group.
Here to write about A,B,C

F/ %
No-200

Sl.No.	Literacy group.	A		B		C	
		Do you know that Labourers are migrating from your village out side the state for livelihood		Whether labourers migrating due to non payment of minimum wages.		Any govt. organisation are making efforts for payment of minimum wages for labourers	
	No. of respondents	Yes	No	Yes	No	Yes	No
1.	Illiterate/110	110/100	0	110/100	0	0	110/100
2.	Middle range educated/36	36/100	0	36/100	0	0	36/100
3	High range educated/54	54/100	0	18/30.33	36/66.67	36/66.67	18/33.33
	Total 200	**200/100**	**0**	**164/82**	**36/18**	**36/18**	**164/82**

Table -6 (D) Basis Age group.
Here to write about A.B.C .

F-%
No-200

Sl.No.	Age group.	A		B		C	
		Do you know that Labourers are migrating from your village all side the state for livelihood		Whether labourers migrating due to non payment of minimum wages.		Any govt. organisation are making efforts for payment of minimum wages for labourers	
	No. of respondents	**Yes**	**No**	**Yes**	**No**	**Yes**	**No**
1.	Upto 30 Yrs/40	40/100	0	40/100	0	0	40/100
2.	31 Yrs to 10 yrs/100	100/100	0	96/96	4/4	4/4	96/96
3.	More than 51 yrs/60	60/100	0	28/46.67	32/53.33	32/53.33	28/46.67
	Total 200	**200/100**	**0**	**164/82**	**36/18**	**36/18**	**164/82**

Table - 6 (A), 6 (B), 6 (C) and 6 (D) is based on different variables each of the table has been divided into three parts related to three different questions of the schedule. In part 'A' of the table Number 6(A) 100% respondents have informed that labourers of the village are migrating from the village out of state for their livelihood. Inpart 'B' of this table 31.25% of F.C. Hindu Muslim 10.72% F.C. Hindu Muslim have informed that labourers are not migrating due to nonpayment of minimum wages. Where as rest of the respondents have informed that labourers are migrating due to nonpayment of minimum wages. In part 'C' of this table 31.25% F.C. Hindu Muslilm, 10.72% B.C. Hindu Muslim have informed that Government organization are making efforts for payment of minimum wages for labourers on the contrary rest of the respondents have informed negatively related to this question.

In part 'A' of table Number 6(B) 100% respondents have informed that labourers are migrating from the village out side the state for livelihood. In part 'B' (of this table 15.63% respondent in Government service 38.75% respondents engaged in agriculture have informed that labourers are not migrating due to nonpayment of minimum wages. Rest of the respondents of all occupation group have informed labourers are migrating due to nonpayment of minimum wages. In part 'C' of this table 15.63% engaged in service, 38.75% engaged in agriculture have informed that Government organization are making efforts for payment of minimum wages for labourers. On the contrary rest of the respondents have informed that Government organization are not making efforts for payment of minimum wages for labourers.

In part 'A'of table Number 6 (C) 100% respondents have informed that labourers are migrating from the village for their livelihood. In part 'B' of this table 66.67% respondent of high range educated have informed the labourers are not migrating due to non-payment of minimum wages on the contrary rest of the respondents of all literacy group have informed that labourers are migrating due to non-payment of minimum wages for labourers,rest of the respondent of all literacy group have informed negatively of this question.

In part 'A' of table number 6 (D) 100% respondents have informed that labourers are migrating from the village for their livelihood. In part 'B' of this table 4% 31 years to 50 years. 53.33% more than 51 years have informed have informed that labourers are migrating not due to nonpayment of minimum wages. Rest of the respondents have informed that labourers are migrating due to nonpayment of minimum wages. In part 'C' of this table 4% 32 years to 50 years of age 53.33% more than 51 years of age have informed that Government organizations are making efforts for payment of minimum wages for labourers. Rest of the respondents have informed that Government organisations are not making efforts for payment of minimum wages for labourers.

Concluding these tables it may be concluded that 100% respondents have informed that labourers of the village are migrating from the village for their livelihood 82% of the respondents have informed that labourers are migrating due to nonpayment of minimum wages and 18% respondents have not felt that labourers are migrating not due to nonpayment of minimum wages.18% respondents have informed that Government organisations are making efforts for payment of minimum wages. Most of the respondents i.e. 82% respondents of the total numberof the respondents have informed that Government organizations are not making efforts for payment of minimum wages for labourers.

Respondents were asked whether economic factor contribute in origin and development of social tension. This question consits of two response categories and the respondents were directed to answer in either of the

Table 7 (A) Basis of Caste group

F/ %
No.200

Sl. No.	Caste group.	A		B If Yes, how?			
	No of Respondents	Does Economic factor contribute in origin and development of tension?		Economic Inequality	Un-employment	Revengeful attitude towards wealthier persons	Govt. development to work like IRDP-20 points programme etc. are not implemented in proper way
		Yes	No				
1.	F.C. Hindu & Muslim/96	76/96.17	20/20.83	76/100	76/100	56/73.68	76/100
2.	B.C.Hindu & Muslim/56	56/100	0	56/100	56/100	56/100	56/100
3.	Low caste/48	48/100	0	48/100	48/100	48/100	48/100
	Total 200	**180/90**	**20/10**	**180/100**	**180/100**	**160/88.89**	**180/100**

Table- 7 (B) Basis Occupation

F-%
No-200

Sl. No.	Occupation group.	A		B If Yes, how?			
	No of Respondents	Does Economic factor contribute in origin and development of tension?		Economic Inequality	Un-employment	Revengeful attitude towards wealthier persons	Govt. development to work like IRDP-20 points programme etc. are not implemented in proper way
		Yes	No				
1.	Labour/70	50/71.42	20/28.58	70/100	70/100	30/60	70/100
2.	Caste Occupation/12	12/100	0	12/100	12/100	12/100	12/100
3.	Business/2	2/100	0	2/100	2/100	2/100	2/100
4.	Service/32	32/100	0	32/100	32/100	32/100	32/100
5.	IndependentOccupation/4	4/100	0	4/100	4/100	4/100	4/100
6.	Agriculture/80	80/100	0	60/100	60/100	80/100	60/100
	Total 200	**180/90**	**20/10**	**180/100**	**180/100**	**160/88.89**	**180/100**

Table No- 7 (C) Basis Literacy group

F-%
N-200

Sl. No.	Literacy group	A		B If Yes, how?			
	No of Respondents	Does Economic factor contribu-te in origin and development of tension?		Economic Inequality	Un-employment	Revengeful attitude towards wealthier persons	Govt. devel-opment to work like IRDP-20 points programme etc. are not implemented in proper way
		Yes	**No**				
1.	Illiterate/100	100/90.91	10/9/09	100/100	100/100	100/100	100/100
2.	Middle range educate/36	28/77.78	8/22.32	28/100	28/100	10/35.71	28/100
3.	High range educated/54	52/96.30	2/3.70	52/100	52/100	50/96.15	52/100
	Total -200	**180/90**	**20/10**	**180/100**	**180/100**	**166/88.89**	**180/100**

Table No- 7 (D) Basis Literacy Gr.

F-%
N-200

Sl. No.	Literacy Gr.	A		B If Yes, how?			
	No of Respondents	Does Economic factor contribu-te in origin and development of tension?		Economic Inequality	Un-employment	Revengeful attitude towards wealthier persons	Govt. devel-opment to work like IRDP-20 points programme etc. are not implemented in proper way
		Yes	**No**				
1.	Illiterate/100	40/100	0	40/100	40/100	40/100	40/100
2.	Middle range educate/36	100/100	0	100/100	100/100	93/93	100/100
3.	High range educated/54	40/66.6	20/33.33	40/100	40/100	50/96.15	40/100
	Total 200	**180/90**	**20/10**	**180/100**	**180/100**	**160/88.89**	**180/100**

category provided to them. In other word t.ey were asked to answer either affirmatively or negatively. Those respondents who answered in category 'Yes' in part 'A' of of the table. They were asked to state as to how economic factors contribute to create and intensify the problem of social tension. The question were provided for response categories to the respondents and they were requested to answer in as much as categories as they liked as it can be seen in the part 'B' of the table. The respones of the respondents with regard to these two questions have been presented in Tabular forms in four tables i.e. Table 7 (A),7(B) 7(C), and (D) on the basis of four different variables.

Each of the table 7 (A) to 7(D) have been divided into two parts i.e. 'A', and 'B' part 'A' of each table shows the number of the respondents who consider economic factors responsible for the creation and acceleration of the problem of social tension.

Part 'A' of the table number 7 (A) shows that economic factors have also been considered responsible for creating this problem. The table shows that 79.19% forward caste group respondents 100% backward caste group respondents. 100% low caste group respondents have informed that economic factors also play a vital role in the creation and acceleration of the problem of social tension. The responses of the respondents with regard to category yes of the table have been found positively co-related to the degree of the status of the castes to which the respondents belong.

Part 'A' of the table number 7 (B) shows that 100% respondents of caste occupation, Business, service, Independent occupation group,agriculturist 71.42% and labour of the total number of the respondents have expressed this view that the economic factors play a vital role so far as the creation and exacerbation of social tension are concerned. However, there is no any significant correlation between occupation and frequency of the respones.

Part 'A' of the table number 7 (C) shows that 90.91% illiterate. 77.78% middle range educated 96.30% High range educated respondents of the total numberof the respondents have expressed this view that economic factors play vital role so far as the creation and exacerbation of social tension is concerned. There is no any co-relation between frequency percentage of the responses and the literacy group. But it is obvous here that high range educated people feel more social tension on the basis of the economic that of middle range educated and illiterate.

Part 'A' of the table - 7 (D) shows that 100% upto 30 years of age, 100% 31 Years to 50 Years of age, 66.67% more than 51 Years of age respondents of the total number of the respondents have expressed this view that the economic factors play vital role as the creation and exacerbation of social tension is concerned. Only 33.33% respondents of more than 51 Years age do not feel social tension on the basis of economy. There is no co-relation between the frequency percentage of responses and age.

Part 'B' of the table -7(A) shows that only 73.66% forward caste of the total number of the respondents who have answered affirmatively in part 'A' of this table here reported that revengeful attitude towards wealthier person is the way through which social tension is createaed. Otherwise 100% respondents of the total number of this table have reported that economic inequality, unemployment revengeful attitude towards wealthier person, Government developmental work like IRDP, 20 points programme and not implemented in proper way are the way through which social tension is created.

Part 'B' of the table -7(B) shows that 60 % labour of the total number of the respondents who have reported affirmatively in part 'A' of this table here reported that revengeful attitude towards wealthier person is the way through which social tension is createaed. Otherwise 100% respondents of the total number of the respondents who reported affirmatively in part 'A' of this table have reported that economic inequality, unemployment, revengeful attitude towards, wealthier person, Government development work like IRDP, 20 points programme are not implemented in proper way are the way through which social tension is created.

Part 'B' of the table -7 (C) shows that 35.71 % middle range educated, 96.15% high range educated respondents of the total numberof the respondents who have answered affirmatively impart 'A' of this table have reported that revengeful attitude towards wealthier person is one of the way of social tension. Whereas 100% respondents of all literacy group of th total numberof the respondents have reported that economic inequality, unemployment, revengeful attitude towards wealtheir persons, Government development programmes, IRDP and 20 points programme etc. are the way through which social tension is created.

Part 'B' of the table -7 (D) shows that 93% 31 Years 50 years of age, 67.5% more than 51 years of the age of the total of the respondents who have answered affirmatively in part 'A' of this table have reported that revangeful attitude towards wealthier persons is one of the way through which social tension is created. Where as 100% respondents of all the groups of the total numberof the respondents have reported that economic inequality, unemployment, revengeful attitude towards wealthier persons, Government development work like IRDP, 20 points programme etc. are not implemented in proper way are the ways through which social tension formed.

Concluding these tables it may be stated that 90% respondents feel that economic factors create social tension. Only 10% respondents do not feel that economic factors created social tension. Only 88.89% respondents of the total numberof the respondents. Who have reported about economic factors as the cause of social tension, have reported that revengeful attitude towards wealthier persons is one of the factors of social tension, Where as 100% respondents of the total number of the respondents who have answered affirmatively about economic factors create social tension have reported that economic inequality, unemployment and government development work like IRDP, 20 points programme etc. are not implemented in proper way are the ways through which social tension is created.

6 SUMMARY AND RECOMMENDATIONS

The present filed work study is partially dedicated towards social tension in rural areas. The Indian leaders are aware of the agrarian or rural tension but inspite of their best efforts and good intentions to solve this tension they have marginally succeeded. The present study is partially dedicated towards that end.

In this field work data from two hundred respondents of Bihara village (village of Saharsa district of North Bihar,) have been collected first of all a list of household head was prepared and then on the basis of caste strata stratfied random sampling was used to select respondents from the sample village. Two methods of structure interview was applied for collecting information related to the problem concerned. The tool of study was schedule (List of question related to problem concerned.)

The present study aims at dinding out the factors of social tension on the basis of economy and providing solution of the problem. The findings of the present study show that—

1. Hundred percent feel economic discrimination between high and low.
2. It shows that each group (on economic basis i.e. landless, landlords, rich poor) is organising against other group.
3. The respondents feel social distance on the basis of economic disparity.
4. It is clear from the findings of this study that forcible acquisition and possession of Bhoodan land and surplus land by landed peasantry has widely offended the feelings of landless people, as they feel that they have been illegally deprived of privileges by the zamindars which were granted to them by the Government.
5. Hundred percent respondents have reported that there is tension between land owner and landless due to nonpayment of minimum wages.
6. The some-what criminal in difference of bureaucracy to effect-

ing payment of minimum wages to the agricultural labour is indirectly aggravating the social tension.

7. That land owners even now want to exploit the labourers though the consciousness of the legitimate rights and privileges of the land labourers has dawned upon the deprived section, nonfulfillment there-of causing further tension.
8. Most of the respondents are of the opinion that economic inequality is a catalyst in formenting social tension in rural India.
9. Related to this economic inequality is the problem of unemployment, under employment or partial employment.
10. A large percentage of respondents view this economic inequality as the basis of animosity which the under privileged section nurtures for the privileged section. Thus deep-rooted ill will erupts and causes social tension.
11. Most of the respondents opine that though the government have launched a number of schemes for the social and economic welfare of specially weaker sections of the society, lackadaisical attitude of government agencies to the implementation of those schemes have instead of creating social harmony, contributed to the creation of social tension as the unprivileged sections believe that they are being discriminated in enjoying the benefits of these schemes.

The findings of this study synchronize with the findings of K.K. Singh, tension in the low castes was found to arise from six sources and conflicts work and related matters such a payment of inadequate wages and extraction of forced labour -inadequate delayed payment for goods and services and from property destruction. The reasons for the similarities for or differences in tension profiles are not to be found in the social or economic status of a caste but rather in the nature of its interaction with the land lord caste. Though this study is related only to economic factor but caste cannot be ignored in the sharer of agrarian scene of India. In the rural areas of India upper and middle caste groups are dominant in economic sphere and on the contrary low caste are the oppressed class.

If we compare the findings of this analysis with the findings of Sachchidanand and K.G. Iyer (1969). It has established co-relation between that attempt on the part of upper caste groups to suppress the aspiration and efforts of the lower castes, situations of conflicts are bound to arise even violence may result. The findings of this analysis also resemble with the finding of Andre Betelle (1969) that land and its harvest has been largely responsible for transforming the conflict between the rich and the poor.

We have so far tried to synchronize on findings that emerge from our study. In the light of above mentioned findings, some recommendations or suggestions could as well be made which may help the policy makers to develop a policy frame to tackle the problem of tension as expressed in the study.

(i) Government and individual should try to minimise the gap between high and low on the basis of economy.

(ii) The Mass literacy programme should be inplemented in proper way so that even the poor should become conscious of their rights and obligations.

(iii) The records of land should be updated.

(iv) Ceiling Act should be implemented in proper way. Surplus land acquired in ceililng should be properly distributed among landless people and their possession should be ensured.

(v) Homestead land should be settled in proper way. More people have been thrown out of their hearth and home after the passing of laws related to homestead land.

(vi) Bataidari act should be implemented in proper way.

(vii) Land which was donated during Bhoodan movement should be properly handed over to landless.

(viii) The act related to minimum wages to rural labour should be strictly implemented. The minimum wage related to agricultural operation should be fixed. On regional basis not on national basis grampanchayat should be empowered to fix minimum wages and implement that accordingly. Payment of minimum wages should be indirect proportion to the work performed. A Yawning gap exists between the actual and the prescribed rate. This has further aggravated strained relationship between land owners and the landless or haves and have nots.

(ix) The role of political parties has been a subject of criticism in all such cases of conflict, violence and tension in rural areas. However, their role should be distinguished from their individal members. We do not subscribe to the view that any party will be officially interested in fomenting rural violence. But I do believe that members of parties may be involved.

(x) This only highlights a very crucial problem in relation to the political socialization of the party members in the norms and values of the over all political system.

(xi) Therefore, the need is to develop a commoncode of conduct among political parties. Such a common code can be built round a consensus on the issue of violence against the weaker sections.Parties must come to agreement that they would not exploit such situations for partisan ends.

(xii) If any political party creates tension and conflicts between people the registration of that particular party should be debarred from contesting elections.

(xiii) The Government should take initiative in organising conferences of party workers at all levels and pose the problem with a view to evolving a consensus. In organising such conferences voluntary organisation can be involved so that the whole affair acquires a non-partis an character.

(xiv) Government should take measure to minimise unemployment and semi-unemployment in the rural areas so that frustration of the mass be minimised, as frustration is the root cause of tension.

(xv) Unionisation of the landless workers should be done. It has been advocated by social thinkers that the government should accelerate the process of bringing the landless and weaker sections in a bargaining position with the land owners. Though some political parties have been involved inorganising unions, somehow every effort at such organisation has led to eruption of violence or tension, thus intensifying the hostility all the more.

(xvi) The government should give adequate powers to Grampanchayats for settling disputes arising out of Bataidari or distribution of surplus land.

(xvii) The Gram Panchayat may also be made financially viable for setting cottage and small scale industries based mainly on agricultures and locally available raw-materials so that empty minds do not turn into devil's den.

(xviii) The Gram Panchayat may also be directed to encourage sports, games and various cultural activities among youth, so that no body will feels neglected. This intermingling or interaction will create emotional harmony which is the appropriate solution of the problem of any type of tension.

(xix) Right to work should be incorporated as fundamental right with certain qualifications and an employment gurantee Act.

BIBLIOGRAPHY

BIBLIOGRAPHY

1. Adams, G.R. (1940): Individual differnces in behaviour resulting from experimentally induced frustration, J.Psy Number, 10

2. Adege, A.R. (1971): Reports on Agriculture Census. Patna Secretariat Press, Bihar.

3. Alexander, P. (1948): Discussion on Hostility and Fear, In social life (by J.Dollard Social Forces Vol. 17).

4. Alexander, V.C.(1975): The Nature and the Background of Agrarian unrest in Kutanal. Indian Journal of Industrial Relations. I

5. Alexander, V.C. (1975): Agrarian Tension in Thanjavur, National Institute of Community Development Hyderabad.

6. Allport, G.W. (1952): Resolution of Intergroup Tensions, New York.

7. Angell, R.C. (1950): Notes on Research and Teaching UNESCO.Social Service Research American Sociological Review, Vol. XV.No.2, April.

8. Avasthi Rajendra, (1975): Psyche, Society and Tension, Minerva Associates, Calcutta.

9. Bateson G, (1941): The Frustration, Aggression Hypothesis and Culture, Psychological Review Vol. 48.

10. Bernard j. :(1951): The Conceptualization of Intergroup Relations, Social Forms Vol.29 No-3.

11.Bihar Legislative, (1954): Vol. 6 No-1, Dec. 13
Assembly Debates

12.Beteille, Andre,(1971): Seminar

13. Beteille, Andre(1971): The Cause of Agrarian Unrest. The Citizen 1, 23

14. Beteille, Andre(1965): Class and power changing patterns of stratification in a Tanjore village university of California Press. Berkeley.

15. Beteille, Andre(1966): Closed and open social stratification in India European Journal of sociology. Vol. VII

16. Beteille, Andre (1969)a: Ideas and Interests some conceptual problems In the study of social Stratification In Rural India. International social Science. Vol. XXI. No-9.

17. Beteille, Andre (1969)b: Decline of Social Inequality (In Social Inequality Selected Reading Harmoners Worth Middlesex.

18. Beteille, Andre (1969)c: Agrarian Unrest In Tanjore, the times of India 20, Sept.

19. Beteille, Andre (1970)a: Peasant Associations and the Agrarian Class Structure. Contribution to Indian Sociology, New series No-IV.

20. Beteille, Andre (1970)b: Implementing Land Reform. The Times of India, 9 Sept.

21. Beteille, Andre (1971): Harmonic and Disharmonic Social Systems. University Press, Sydney.

22. Beteille, Andre(1972): Inequality and Social Change, Oxford University Press.

23. Berman, Y, (1974)a: Mobilization of Landless Labourers Halpatis of South Gujarat E.P.W9 (12)

24. Berman, Y, (1974) b: Patronage and Exploitation. Changing Agrarian Relation In South Gujarat, Berkeley University of California press.

25. Bergal Egon Ernest, (1962): Social Stratification, New York.

26. Berkowitz.L: (1962): Aggression Hill, Book Company, New York.

27. Bhaskaran, R. (1967): Sociology of Politics, Bombay, Asia Publishing House.

28. Bharadwaj, K.(1976): Understanding Rural Social Change Review of E.Whitcombe's Agrarian conditions In North India Vol-I The United Provinces under British Rule 1860-1900,Berkeley University of California Press E.P.W.11(8).

29. Bhaduri, A, (1973): A Study in Agricultural Backwardness under semi Feudalism, Economic Journal, LXXX VI 329.

30. Bhalla Sheela, (1977): Agricultural Growth Rule of Institutional and Infrastructural Factors, E.P.W. Vol. XII NO-45-46.

31. Brend, W.O, (1944): The Foundation of Human Conflict, London.

32. Brker, R (1941): Rrustration and Fegression, unive.La.stud.child, welf. No-1

33. Broom Field,J.H. (1966): Elite Conflict in a Plural Society, Twentieth Century, Bengal.

34. Buckly,William, (1959): Social Stratification and the Functional Theory of Social Defferentiation American Sociological Review, 23(3).

35. Cantrill, H. (1950): (Ed) Tensions that Cause Wars.

36. Carter, T.A. (1974): Elite Politics in Rural India. Cambridge University press.

37. Cameron (1947): The Psychology of Behaviour Disorder, Copy Right.

38. Chandra,N.K. (1974): Farm efficiency under semi Feudalism A Critique of Morginalist Theories & Some Marxist Formulations.E.P.W.IV (32,33,34).

39. Chakravarti, Anand (1986): Economic and Political Weekly.

40. Chandra,N.K. (1975), ABC: Agrarian Transition In India- in three parts, Frontier VI No-28,29,30.

41. Chandra, B.(1974): Some Aspects of Indian Village Society, Indian History Review No-151-64

42. Chandra, B. (1966): The Rise and Growth of Economic Nationalism in India, Delhi,People's Publishing House.

43. Choudhary, R.K. (1976): Cultural Heritage of Mithila, Indira Gandhi Abhinandan Granth, Vol.II

44. Choudhary, P.C.Roy, (1954): Bihar District Gazetteer, Saharsa Secretariat Press, Patna.

45. Chattopadhyay, P. (1972) a: On the question of the Mode of Production In Indian Agriculture, E.P.W. VII(13)39-46.

46. Chattopadhyay, P. P. (1972) b: Mode of Agriculture Antikritik E.P.W. VII 185-92.

47.Chattopadhyay, P.(1980): Mode of Production In Indian Agriculture and Afterward,E.P.WXV 85-8,

48. Cohn Bernard, And Singer, M: (ed) — Structure and Change In Indian Society, Chicago Aldine, Publishing Company.

49. Coser, L.H. (1956): — The Foundations of Social Conflict, London.

50. Dahrendorf, R.(1958): — Towards A Theory of Social Conflict, The Journal of Conflict Resolution, June.

51. Davies, J.C. (1970) — Towards Theory of Resolution,Princeton New Jersey.

52. Dankebar, V.M. Khudonpur, G.S.: (1948), — Working of Bombay Tenancy Act Report.

53. Das Gupta, Biplob, 1977: — India's Green Revolution.E.P.W.XII (6,7,8) Feb.

54. Das and Nandi (1985): — Violence Victimhood and the Language of Silence, In Contribution to Indian Sociology (N.S.)19(1) 177.218.

55. Davitz. J.R. (1942): — The effects of previous training on post frustration behaviour, J.Abnorm. Soc.Psy.47

56. Delight, B.(1937): — Congress of Voilence, London.

57. Desai and Mehta, (1969): — Rural Sociology in India, Bombay Popular Prakashan.

58. Desai and Mehta, (1979)a: — Peasant Struggle in India,Bombay popular Prakashan.

59. Desai and mehta, (1979)a: — Rural India In Transition,Bombay, Popular Prakashan.

60. Desai, A.R.(ed.) (1959): — Rural Sociology in India, Bombay Popular Prakashan.

61. Dolland, J. and others, (1939): Frustraration and Aggression, New Haven.

62. Dollard, J. (1944): Frustration and Aggression, London.

63. Dorsey, J.M. (1951): A Psychotherapeutic Approach to the Problem of Hostility, Social Forces, Vol.29 No 3 March.

64. D.Souza, V. (1981): Inequality and Its Perpetuation. A Theory of Social Stratification, New Delhi, Manohar.

65. Durheim, E, (1960): (Tr. by Cr.Simpson) The Division of Labour In Society.

66. Dubey, S.C. (1959): Indian Village, Routledge and Kegan Paul.

67. Dubey, S.C. (1958): India's Changing villages, London, Rutledge and Kegan Paul.

68. Dutta,Sunanda, K-(1980): Harijan on the March, Statesmen, March -II.

69. Feirchild,H.P.(1967): The Dictionary of Sociology,New Jersey

70. Fierabend Rosaling, (1972): Social Change and Political Violence, New Jersay Cross National pattern and Prentice Hall.

71. Fisraband Ivok, (1972): Angel Violence and Politics, New Jersey Prentice Hall I.N.C.

72. Frank, A.G. (1970): The Wealth and Poverty of Nations, E.P.W.

73. Freud, S. (1915): New Introductory letures on Psycho Analysis, Norton,New York, 29-31.

74. Gadgill, D.K. (1969): Two Powerful Classes In Agrarian Areas (ed) Rural Sociology In India, Bombay Popular Prakashan.

75. Galenter, Mare, (1961): Eqality and Protective Discrimination In India, Rutgers Law Review 16 (1).

76. Ghurye, G.S. (1968): Social Tension in India, Bombay Popular Prakashan.

77. Ghosh K. (1969): Agricultural Labourers in India.

78. Ghosh K. (1969): Agriculture Labour in Calcutta Indian Publication.

79. Govt of India, (1969): The Causes and Nature of Current Agrarian Tension, Ministry of Home Affairs, New Delhi.

80. Gough, K, (1969): Peasant Resistance and Revolt In South India Pacific Affairs 41(4) 526-544.

81. Goode and Hatt, P.K. (1952): Methods In Social Research Mcgraw Hill, New York Book Co. I.N.C

82. Gupta, S.C. (1969): Some Aspects of Indian Agriculture (ed) A.R.Desai Rural Sociology.

83. Guthree, E.R. (1938): The Psychology of Human Conflict, London.

84. Curr, T.R. (1970): Why Man Rebel, Prentice Hall, New Jersey, Engle Wood Cliff.

85. Curr, T.R. (1972): Psychological Factors In Civil Violence, Prentice Hall, Y.H.C. New Jersey, Engle Wood Pliff.

86. Harriman. P.I. (1944): The New Dictionary of Psychology. New York.

87. Hageu, E.E, (192): On the Theory of Social Change, the Dorsal Press, Illinbis.

88. Haksar Nandita, (1983): Justice for common Man, The Hindustan - Times, May, 22

89. Harper, E.B. (1959): The System of Economic Exchange in Village India American Anthropologist Vol. LXI.

90. Harriman, P.L. (1946) (ed): Encyclopaedia of Psychology, New York.

91. Harriman, P.L. (1974): The New Dictionary of Psychology, New York.

92. Hauington, S.P.,(1969): Political Order in Changing Societies, New Haven, Yale University Press.

93. Hiraman, A.B. (1977): Social Change in Rural India, B.R. Publications.

94. Hindustan (Daily Hindi) (1991): 29 March (Newspaper)

95. Horny, K, (1946): Our Inner Conflict, London.

96. Huyler, Stephenp (1985): Village India I.N.C. Publishers New York.

97. India Today, (1989): October 31

98. Indradeep Singh, (1967): The Search Light, October 8

99. Indradeep Singh, (1968): Main Stream Vol. VI,No-25 February, 17

100. Ishwaran, K, (1966): Tradition and Economy In Village India, Routeledge and Kegan Paul.

101. Ishwaran, K, (1970): Change and Continutiy In India's village, New York, Columbia University press.

102. Jackson J.A.(1968): Social Stratification,Cambridge University Press.

103. Jannauzi, F.T., (1974): Agrarian Crisis in India, New Delhi Sangam Books.

104. Jannauzi, F.T., (1978): Problems of Land Reforms in the second stage presented to the Round Table on Adaptation of Administration to Rural development.

105. Joshi, P.C. (1971)a: Land Hunger,Delhi, Seminar, April.

106. Joshi, P.C.(1971)b: Land Reform and Agrarian Change in India and Pakistan since 1947 II Journal of Peasant (Report) Studies 1(3) 326-62.

107. Joshi, P.C. (1975): Land Reform in Trend and perspective Bombay Allied Pub.Ltd.

108. Joshi, P.C. (1970): Review Article, Delhi, Seminar. May.

109. Joshi, P.C. (1974): Review Article, Delhi, Seminar.

110. Kane, J.J. (1951): Protestant Catholic Tension, American sociological Review.

111. Karna, M.N.(1975): Agrarian Tension and Violence, Journal of Social and Economic Studies III, 1,34.

112. Kretch, and Crutch Field, R.E.(1962): Individual in Society, New York Mc. Graw Hill Book Company, September.

113. Khushro, A.M. (1958): Economic and Social Effects of Jagirdari Abolition and Land Reform in Hyderabad.

114. Kishor, Surendra, (1975): The Massacre of Agricultural labour in the Name of Naxals, Pratipaksh, June, 8.

115. Klineberg,O,(1950): Tension Affecting International Understanding, New York.

116. Kotovsky G. (1964): Agrarian Reforms in India, Delhi.

117. Kotovsky, G: (1964): Agrarian Reform in India,Bombay people's publishing House.

118. Karna, M.N., (1981): Agrarian Structure and Peasant Mobilization Sociological Bulletin. Vo. 30 Novemebr-2

119. Kumar Prasant, (1981): Kisan Andolan, Dharmyug, Hindi Weekly, 24 May

120. Kurushetraya, (1985): May.

121. Kuppuswamy, B,(1967): Socio-Economic Status Stratification in Western U.P. Sociological Bulletin March, 16 (1)

122. Kuppuswamy, B,(1972): Social Change in India, Bombay Asia Pub.House

123. Ledejinsky, W, (1964): Agrarian Reform in Asia,Foreign Affairs April.

124. Lasminarayan,H.D, (1976): India's village At Cross Road, Delhi, National

125. Lewis Occer, (1958): Life in a North Indian village, University of Ilinoy's press Alabama.

126. Lewin, K, (1948): Resolving Social Conflicts, New York.

127. Lewin K. and Others, (1955): Authority and Frustration,Iowa.

128. Lenski, G.E.(1966). Power and privileges a Few Theory of Stratification, Mograw Hill.

129. Maine Sir, H, (1980): Village Communitiesin the East and west
Maier, N.R.F. (1940): Studies of abnormal behaviour J. Exp.Psy.26 London.

130. Majumdar, D.N., (1959): Inter Caste Tension (In Rural Sociology in India Ed.,A.R. Desai.)

131. Marx, Karl, (1956): Contribution to the Critique of Political Economy.

132. Mac.Dougall, W, (1921): The Group mind, Cambridge.

133. Martin, E.D. (1932): The Conflict of the Individual and the Mass in the Modern world, New York.

134. Marriott Mackim, (1961): Village India (Ed), Bombay Asia Pulishing house,

135. Malviya, H.D. (1955): Land Reform in India (A.R.Desia (Ed.) Rural Sociology in India, Bombay Popular Pakashan.

136. Mencher, J, (1970): Change Agents and Villagers,An Analysis of their Relationship and the Role of Class Values, E.P.W.V. 1187-87

137. Mencher, J, (1974): Conflict and contradictions in the Green Revolution the Case of Tamil Nadu E.P.W.9(6,7,8) 309-23.

138. Mencher, J, (1974): Agricutlure and Social Structure in Tamil Nadu, New Delhi, Allied

139. Mencher, J, (1980): The Lessons and Mass Lessions of Kerala Agriculture Labourers and Poverty, E.P.W. 1781-1802.

140. Mehta Uday, (1969): The Problem of the Marginal Farmers in India Agriculture (In A.K. Desia Ed, Rural Sociology in India, Bombay Popular Prakashan.)

141. Ministry of Agriculture (1978) : Deptt.of Rural Development Government of India Report The Committe on Panchayati Raj Insitituation (New Delhi of Andhra Press)

142. Mishra, B.B.(1961): The Indian Middle Classes, London

143. Mowrer, O.H. (1938): Frustration and Aggression, New Haven, Yale University Press

144. Mukerji Kalayan and Yadav Rajendra Singh: (1980), Bhojpur-Naxlism in the Plain of Bihar, Delhi, Radha Kamal Prakashan.

145. Mukherji, P.N. (1978): Naxl bari Movement and Peasant Revolt in North Bengal in M.S.A. Rao (ed) Social Movement in India Vol, I, New Delhi, Manohar.

146. Mukerji Ram Krishna, (1957): The Dynamic of a Rural Society: a Study of the Economic Structure in Bengal villages, Berlin, Akademic verley.

147. Mukherji, Radha Kamal and Mishra, S.D. (1955) Inter Caste Tensions in India.

148. Murphy, G.(1947): Personality and Bio-Social Approach to Origin and Structure, New York.

149.Myrdal Gunnar, (1968): Asian Drama in Inquiry into the poverty of Nations, Penguine Books, Vol.I

150.Natrajan, S. (1959): Century of Social Reform in India Bombay, Asia Publishing House.

151. Namboodaripad, (1979): Caste Conflicts Vs. Growing Unity of popular Democratic Forces, Economic and political Weekly, 17(7,8,) 329-36.

152. National Sample Survey: No.30, 122, 146

153. Neal Watter, C.(1967): Economic Changes in Rural India Hand Tenure and Reform in Utter Pradesh 1600-(1966) Yale University Press.

154. New Comb.I.B. (1947): (Ed.) Reading in Social Psychology New York.

155. New Age, (1967): October 15.

156. Namboodaripad, E.M.S. (1952): Public Address Bombay

157. Omvedt; G.(1978): Towards a Marxist Analysis of Caste Social Scientist VI(II) 70-6.

158. Omvedt; G. (1981): Capitalist Agriculture and Rural Classes in India, Economic and Political Weekly XVI 52 (140-59).

159. Oomen, T.K, (1970): Non Violent Approach to Land Reforms. The Case of An Agrarian Movement in India.

160. Oomen, T.K, (1971): Agrarian Tension in Kerala District. An analysis, Indian Journal of Industrial Relations 7(2).

161. Oomen, T.K, (1971): Green Revolution and Agrarian Conflict, E.P.W; Vol.26 June 20.

162. Oomen, T.K, (1975): Agrarian Legislations and Movements As Source of change, E.P.W.V 40 Oct.4.

163. Oomen, T.K, (1984): Social Transformation in Rural India Mobilizatin and State intervention, Delhi, Vikas.

164. Patnaik, (1971): Capitalist Development in Agriculture, E.P.W. VI(39) 123-30.

165. Patnaik, (1972): Development of Capitalisam in Agriculture, Social Scientist, 15-31

166. Patnaik, (1976): Class Differentiation within the Peasantry an Approach to Analysis of Indian Agriculture E.P.W. XI (39) 82-101.

167. Patwardhan, S., (1973): Change Among Indian Harijans, Delhi, Orient Longman.

168. Prasad, N, (1970): Change Strategy in Developing Society, Meerut, Menakshi Prakashan.

169. Prasad, P.H. (1975): Agrarian Unrest and Economic Change in Rural Bihar, E.P.W. 10(24)

170. Prasad, P.H. (1976): Poverty and Bandage, Economic and Political Weekly Sept. No, 11(31-33) 1268-72

171. Prasad, P.H. (1979): Caste and Class in Bihar E.P.W.XIV (7 & 8) 481-4.

172. Prasad, P.H. (1980): Rising Middle Peasantry in North India, E.P.W.XV(5,6,&7) 225-79.

173. Planning Commission, (1973): Tasks Force on Agrarian Relations Report, New Delhi.

174. Rao V.K.R.V. (1985): The Current Crisis in darkness Before Down, Allahabad, Vohra Publishers and Distributors.

175. Ram, Nandu, (1977): Social Mobility and Social Conflict in Rural U.P.,Indian Anthropologst, 7(2), 11-24.

176. Rath, R.K., (1979): The Green Revolution Promise and Problems, Kurukshetra, Vol.XXVII No-20 July 16th.

177. Rastogi, P.N., (1968): Polarization, Politics and Economics in Rural Life in East U.P. Indian Journal of Social Work.

178. Rastogi, P.N., (1975): The Nature and Dynamic of Factional Conflict, Meerut, Macmillan Co, India.

179. Raj Gopal, P.R. (1987): Social Change and Violence, New Delhi,Uppal Publication, New Delhi

180. Ravivar Weekly,(1980): Garib Kishan

181. Redfield, R., (1956): Peasant Society and Culture, Chicago, The University of Chicago Press.

182. Report U.P. Zamindari (1978): Abolition Commitee.

183. Rudra, Ashok, (1978): Class Relation in Indian Agriculture, E.P.W. VIII(22,23 & 24) 916-23, 963-68,998-1003.

184. Rudra, Ashok, (1981): Against Feudalisam E.P.W.XVI (52) 2733-46

185. Ruch, F.L. (1955): Psychology and life scott, foreman and Company

186. Sachchidanand and Iyer, K.G. (1969): Caste Tension in Patna Bastern Anthropologist Vol.XXII No-3, September December.

187. Sanford, F.H. (1961): Psychology, A scientific study of man, Words Worth Publishing Company San Francisco

188. Sen Gupta, Bhowani (1962): Evolution of Agrarian Relation in India, New Delhi people's publishing house.

189. Sen, Gupta N., (1977): Further on the Mode of Production in Agriculture E.P.W. (Supplement) 12(26) A 55 A 63.

190. Sen, Sunil, (1976): Agrarian Change in Punjab, Mainstream 14, Annual No.

191. Sharma Dr. Brahmadeo, (1989): Report of the Commissioner for Scheduled Caste and Scheduled tribe for period ending 31.10.1989 Ministry of Home Affairs, New Delhi.

192. Sharma, H. (1974): From Factionalism to Class Polarization The Eastern Anthropologist, 27(2).

193. Sharma, R.D. (1965): Indian Feudalism C 300-1200, Delhi Macmillan.

194. Sharma, K.L., (1974): The Changing Rural Stratification System, New Delhi, Orient Longman.

195. Sharma, K.L., (1980): Essays on Social Stratification, Jaipur Rawat.

196. Sharma K.L., (1983): Agrarian Stratification E.P.W.18 (42,43).

197. Shah, A.M., (1969): Rural Class Structure in Gujarat, (A.R. Desai (ed) Rural Sociology in India.)

198. Simie, J.N. (1969): Citizen in Country, (Patterns of Caste Tension by K.K. Singh as quoted)

199. Smith, K.U. (1958): The Behaviour of Man, Henry Holt and Company.

200. Singh, Durganand, (1969): The Indian Village in Transition, New Delhi, Associate.

201. Singh Arun, (1980): Land Grab Caste Rifle Behind Violence Indian Express, February 10.

202. Singh, Rajendra, (1974): Agrarian Social Structure and Peasant Unrest, Sociological Bulletin 23,1.

203. Singh, Yogendra, (1958): Next Step in Village India, Bombay, Asia Publishing House.

204. Singh, Yogendra, (1958): The Changing Pattern of Socio-Economic Relations in the Country side, Phd, Lucknow University.

205. Singh,Yogendra,(1969):Changing Power Structure of Village Community (In A.R. Desai Rural Sociology in India, Bombay Popular Prasashan.)

206.Singh,Yogendra,(1977): Social Stratification and Change in India, New Delhi, Manohar.

207.Singh, Yogendra, (1993): Social Change in India, Delhi, Har Anand Publications.

208. Somaji, A.H. (1970): Democracy and Political Change in Village India, Bombay Orient Longman.

209. Sorokin, P.A., (1937): Democracy and Political Change in Village India, Bombay, Orient Longman.

210. Srinivas, M.N., (1955): India's Villages, Bombay, Asia Publishing House.

211. Srinivas, M.N., (1964): The Study of Dispute, Bombay, Asia Publishing House.

212. Stokes, Eric, (1978): The Peasant and The Raj, New Delhi, Vikas.

213. Symonds, P.M.(1946): The Dynamics of Human Adjustement. New York.

214. Thompson, E.P. (1978): The Poverty of the Theory and other Essays, London, arting Press.

215. Thorner, Danieal, (1969): Land Reforms (In A.R.Desai (ed) Rural Sociology in India, Bombay Popular Prakashan.)

216. The New Dictionary of psychology: (1947): Philosphical Library, New York.

217. The Times of India: June 9th (1980), Feb, 19th, (1980), Oct.-24th (1989):

218. The Indian Nation: March 13th, 1956, Nov.13th (1967):

219. The Search Light: Nov.24th, 1955, Oct. 23rd (1967), Dec-7th (1967): Nov.13th (1967).

220. Townseed Peter, (1965): The Meaning of Poverty, British Journal of Sociology 13 (3).

221. Tumin, Malvin, M, (1953): Some Principles of Statification American Sociological Review 18(4).

222. Tumin, Malvin, M, (1963): On Inequality, American Sociological Revew February 28 (1).

223. Tumin, Malvin, M, (1967): Social Stratification, New Jersey, Englewood Cliffs.

224. Under Wood, B.J. (1949): Experemental Psychology, New York, Century Crofts. New York.

225. Vivekanand, Swami, (1963): India and Her problem, Advaita Ashram, Calcutta.

226. Warren, H.C. 1934: Dictionary of Psychology, New York.

227. Warriner, Dorren (1969): Land Reform in Principle and Practice Oxford.

228. Weber Max, (1952): Essays in Sociology, Routledge and Kegan Paul Ltd.

229. Weiner, Myron,(1963): The Politics of Scarcity, Bombay, Asia Pub.House.

230. William, R.M. (1947): The Reduction of Intergroup Tension, New York.

231. Wright, Quincy,(1944): The Study of War, 2 Vols,Chicago.

232. Wright, Quincy, (1950): The Importance of the Study of Internal Tensions International UNESCO, Vol.11 No1

233. Wood Evelgan, (1964): Caste, Latest Image, Economic Weekly 16 (14)

234. Yojana, (1985): Vol.290 Oct.1.

235. Yojana, (1978). Oct. Nov.

INDEX